the driving people

The CHANGING Driver's Handbook
Your guide to fuel efficient driving techniques and car choice

Also from Veloce Publishing –

Electric Cars – The Future is Now! (Linde)
Roads with a View – England's greatest views and how to find them by road
(Corfield)

www.rac.co.uk
www.veloce.co.uk

This publication has been produced on behalf of RAC by Veloce Publishing Ltd.
The views and the opinions expressed by the author are entirely his own, and do
not necessarily reflect those of RAC. New automotive technology is constantly
emerging; the information in this book reflects the status quo at the date of
publication.

First published in August 2010 by Veloce Publishing Limited, Veloce House,
Parkway Farm Business Park, Middle Farm Way, Poundbury, Dorchester, Dorset,
DT1 3AR, England.
Fax 01305 250479/e-mail info@veloce.co.uk/web www.veloce.co.uk or
www.velocebooks.com.

ISBN: 978-1-845843-51-9 UPC: 6-36847-04351-3

the driving people

The Efficient Driver's Handbook
Your guide to fuel efficient driving techniques and car choice

Dave Moss

Contents

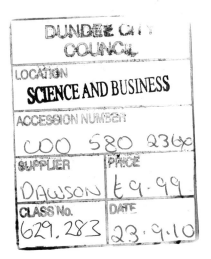

Foreword

Few vehicle drivers today can remain unaware of the direct link between consumption of the world's non-renewable supplies of oil, exhaust pollution, and the ever-growing number of internal combustion engines on which the vast majority of our vehicles, big and small, rely so heavily. Perhaps less well appreciated, however, is another direct link: between a vehicle's fuel consumption, its emissions – and the driver behind the steering wheel.

With the ever-rising cost of fuel today, more and more drivers are discovering that a thoughtful choice of vehicle, coupled with a considered approach when using it, can directly result in significant benefits. Whether a vehicle is used privately or on business, the most obvious of these is a consistent and tangible saving in cash spent on fuel. Perhaps unsurprisingly, this more efficient approach to vehicle use, and indeed purchase, is attracting more and more converts to the efficient driving cause every day – but of course, there is very much more to this issue than just cash. Eco-driving techniques help towards improved road safety, and the reduced exhaust emissions which are another beneficial result have an impact on securing a cleaner environment for all of us, and our children, in the future.

At heart, efficient, eco-driving techniques might seem simple enough. Yet, like all life's most practical skills, the secrets of real success are founded on a wide-ranging understanding of the topic: a combination of background knowledge, explanations, insight, some training, encouragement, experience – and dedication. It's all in this book, as is a look at the way ahead, towards ever-more efficient driving as the future unfolds.

RAC

Acknowledgements

Thanks go to a long list of people who have contributed encouragement, advice, observations. information and ideas over a period of years as this book has progressed from an idea to a finished work.

In particular, some of the many include John Kendall, Peter Gimber, Mike Hull, Lesley Smith, Ross Durkin, Tony Aspinall, Jeremy Phillips, Reg Burnard and Martyn Gould.

Most photographs in this book are from the author's collection, or were taken to demonstrate or clarify points arising in the text. Special thanks to Reg Burnard and Glen Smale for their help in locating and providing a number of photographs in section 2.

Introduction

Most car drivers today seem to feel that the cost of petrol and diesel is too high.

Most also accept and admit, usually with more than a tinge of guilt, that their use of a car is resulting in pollution of the atmosphere. Yet, judged on the standard of driving seen daily on our roads, few drivers seem to recognise the solid and direct link between their everyday driving style, the distance travelled on the fuel they purchase for the vehicle, and the exhaust emissions it creates. Fuel prices are heading ever upwards, but you can lessen the impact of those spiralling prices by understanding and applying the efficient, economical driving techniques contained in this book.

If you can make that fuel go further, your wallet or purse will be a clear beneficiary: but in these enlightened times driving efficiently and economically brings other benefits besides saving money on your motoring. It's also about improved safety on the road and in playing a part in bigger, long-term issues, through an informed choice of vehicle, and minimising exhaust pollution – in turn making a contribution to the wellbeing of future generations and our planet in general.

Since cash in today's society is king, let's get back to basics, and that economical driving payback. If your car currently averages 30mpg, and this book encouraged you to adopt a more economical driving style resulting in a 10 per cent saving in fuel used, you'll travel another 3 miles for each gallon of fuel purchased. It may not sound a lot, but just try walking it ... A saving of 10 per cent means that, for every 10 gallons (approximately 45 litres) of fuel you buy – a typical tankful in many smaller vehicles – you'll get a 'free' gallon of fuel ... That's a pretty good result, which, for a driver covering 10,000 miles a year, amounts to 33 'free' gallons (approx 150 litres) in 12 months.

And no, this fuel saving is not

a flight of fancy: an overall 3mpg improvement is perfectly possible for drivers of typical mainstream cars in today's driving conditions. Depending on your car, and how you presently drive, you might achieve more than that – particularly if it's diesel-engined. Even a 20 per cent improvement is not out of the question, but much will depend on your current driving style, and when, where and how far you drive. Van drivers, incidentally, are by no means immune to such improvements, and because most light commercials are nowadays diesel-powered and often hard-driven, the fuel saving potential can be very significant.

Better economy in today's motoring climate convincingly saves cash, and simultaneously brings that built-in contribution to saving the planet – through the gilt-edged bonus of reduced emissions. If you burn petrol, diesel or any other fossil fuel directly to move a vehicle, the engine unavoidably produces a range of undesirable pollutants, which head into the atmosphere through the exhaust pipe. The principal culprits here are hydrocarbons and carbon monoxide, nitrogen oxides and particulates. Though you may well have heard of some of these, the link between fuel consumption and emissions of such substances is not as strong as it is with the greenhouse gas carbon dioxide – CO_2 – which is probably today's best known, and most infamous, tailpipe pollutant. The quantity of CO_2 generated links directly to the type and amount of fuel consumed. For most other pollutants actual levels are more dependent on such things as vehicle age, technology and design, engine maintenance, and even seemingly unrelated matters like the ambient temperature.

Whatever its chemical name, today the pollution generated by internal combustion engines burning the most common fuels – petrol or diesel – tends to be largely invisible, but in these environmentally enlightened times it really cannot forever be a case of 'out of sight, out of mind.'

In general, the more fuel burnt, the more pollution is generated, though the composition of the pollution will differ depending on the fuel in use. A typical petrol-engined car achieving our hypothetical 30mpg might emit 180 grams of CO_2 per kilometre travelled – over 8.6 kilograms every 30 miles. A long-term 10 per cent reduction in consumption resulting from a new-found, more economical driving style would reduce those emissions pro-rata, equating to a significant CO_2 emissions reduction during a single year's motoring.

Diesel CO_2 emissions with an otherwise similar vehicle will normally be lower for the distance driven, but that's really no good reason to avoid driving a diesel vehicle in a more economical way wherever possible.

In an age when a private car is seen as a necessity for many, and the costs of keeping it running are centre stage, understandably your mind may be focussed more on saving cash than on saving the planet. Yet the fact is today – like never before – the world's ecology needs people like us: drivers determined to drive more economically – and more efficiently. Achieving an environmental turnaround for future generations relies on more and more of us doing what we can to make a real difference ...

Though the fuel our vehicles use may change in coming years, motorised transport seems likely to be a cornerstone of civilisation for a while longer yet – and magic technical panaceas to combat the production of both greenhouse gas and other vehicle pollutants are still in pretty short supply. Today's increasingly sophisticated, catalyst- and particulate-filter equipped vehicles are helping, but the practical, carbon-based vehicle fuel that does not deplete the worlds resources – or pollute the world's atmosphere – does not exist. Ultimately, the oil we refine to fuel so much of our civilisation's energy demands will run out.

Whilst much of this book concentrates on the practical things a driver can do to make every journey more ecologically – and hopefully more financially – efficient, the motoring world about us is steadily changing. As we shall see in chapter 3, long-familiar petrol and diesel fuels are now complemented by both blended and alternative options – both of which are of potential interest to drivers determined to be more efficient. Moreover, new forms of vehicle propulsion are either with us now or on the horizon and which, through improved mechanical efficiency, can improve fuel economy while offering reduced exhaust pollution. Some such solutions are promising, and through considerable – if occasionally controversial – ecological advantages, may well provide a useful stepping stone to a still distant future of genuine 'zero emission' vehicles.

Efficient drivers may well recognise an important point of differentiation here – the future ideal is surely for vehicles to be truly zero emitting over their full operational cycle, whatever fuel is used. This is markedly different from zero emitting at the point of actual use, where the emissions involved in providing motive power are diverted away from the vehicle but occur somewhere else – usually a power generating facility – which with today's technology is highly unlikely to be zero emitting.

With growing vehicle use, steady depletion of the world's finite oil resources and atmospheric pollution all irrevocably linked, it's long been within the grasp of every driver to become more efficient, Today, the incentives have never been higher. Hopefully, this book will provide the motivation and information to allow the reader to start, continue and develop an efficient and economical driving style, which as time passes will become second nature. It should also provide an insight to the whys and wherefores of driving for efficiency, and the informed choices that drivers can already make – as well as offer a brief, accessible look at some of the anticipated problems of the future as they relate to alternative vehicle fuels and power sources.

None of what follows is rocket science. Indeed, some of it might seem painfully obvious, but the simple fact is that driving efficiently for economy does work. Therefore, the opportunity exists for every vehicle user to help the common cause of working for a cleaner, more sustainable future.

If you genuinely want to spend less on fuel, and help minimise damage to the environment – don't delay. You've bought the book, now it's time to seize the opportunity! It'll take a little effort, strong will, a new focus on motoring life for both today and tomorrow, and, ultimately, long-term determination. You'll also find yourself reconsidering your state of mind, and contemplating other drivers' state of mind too. However. the inescapable fact is you, yes YOU, genuinely can make a difference. You'll be saving money, helping the planet, and you'll be a better, safer driver for it.

Enough talk: lets get started!

Dave Moss

one

Choosing an efficient and economical car

Ground rules on fuel economy and exhaust emissions

Let's start with a truism: no matter the type of fuel or size of vehicle, stretching whatever fuel is used to cover the furthest possible distance ensures that emissions over that distance are reduced as far as possible. A steady rise in the number of alternative ways of powering vehicles has complicated things slightly, but still the fundamental concept remains: the less primary, carbon-based fuel consumed – at any stage – the lower the emissions will be.

At the time of writing, one of the several so-called 'hybrid' cars on sale is likely to reward its driver with both the lowest exhaust emissions and the most economical drive, in terms of the size of the car and quantity of fuel consumed. Yet hybrids are complex cars, mostly coming at premium prices, and their economy and low emissions at the point of use are, to some extent, being challenged by advanced

but 'conventional' designs. Hybrids also come with some less obvious disadvantages, which we will consider later.

In general, amongst what are still regarded as conventional cars, best economy and low emissions are at their optimum in small, modestly-powered vehicles, which are light in weight and as mechanically efficient as possible. Generally, less fuel is used in accelerating a small, light, uncomplicated car to any particular speed, and less power is needed to keep it there.

Whilst the economy differential is less marked amongst smaller cars – some of today's petrol engines can deliver beyond 50mpg in real-world driving conditions – diesel-powered cars tend to be more economical in use, generally. This is because a diesel engine has potential inherent in its design to stretch fuel further. However, it's important to recognise that running costs associated with diesel cars can often be higher, eating into any savings made on fuel economy.

Diesel fuel can sometimes be more expensive per litre than petrol, and diesel cars usually have a higher initial purchase price. They may also need more frequent workshop servicing, and their engine oil may need replacing more often. However, properly maintained diesel engines also have a formidable reputation for covering very high mileages without complaint, which can significantly slow a vehicle's overall rate of depreciation. All these things are worthy of careful consideration quite separately from outright fuel economy – this will balance a cost-based decision on whether to opt for a petrol or diesel car. There's little point selecting a diesel vehicle on the basis of fuel consumption of, say, 10mpg better than its petrol-powered equivalent, if the mileage you will be covering is so low that it will take more years than you intend to keep the vehicle just to recover the extra initial outlay of buying and maintaining the diesel version. You might still decide to go with the diesel on the basis of lower CO_2 emissions, perhaps, but it's well worth doing a few sums before splashing out on a new car to avoid making a costly long-term mistake.

Whatever the size or type of vehicle, or its method of propulsion, its aerodynamics play a major and often unappreciated part in fuel efficiency. Whilst it might appear that smaller cars will be naturally more aerodynamic than larger ones, this is not automatically the case. A small car may well have a smaller frontal area to 'bore' through the atmosphere, which is important, but this is really just one factor in a very complex science. For instance, it is generally easier to design low wind-resistance into larger cars, but other,

unrelated factors will still make them less fuel efficient overall. Any vehicle body design, big or small, can be optimised for reduced wind resistance, a characteristic explored and exploited more frequently today in the light of growing legislative and consumer demands for ever-better efficiency.

Some manufacturers routinely tailor the body designs of selected small to mid-size cars to deliberately reduce aerodynamic drag – the resistance the vehicle encounters as it moves through the atmosphere. Along with engine and other changes, such tailoring means a more eco-efficient version of the standard model can be offered, usually at a premium price. Although outwardly often closely resembling the vehicle from which they have been developed, such designs can pay distinct economy and emissions gains, though sometimes there are minor driveability foibles.

Before buying a vehicle of this type, it will certainly be worth evaluating the mileage you will cover against your intended length of ownership to ensure not only that a higher list price is fully recouped, but also that tangible savings will be made during your time with the car. These will become more apparent as usage creeps towards 12,000 miles per annum, particularly if the vehicle has a diesel engine.

Generally, a five- or six-speed manual gearbox and front-wheel-drive is likely to be more fuel-efficient than an automatic or a 4x4 drivetrain in transmitting available power to the road. However, motor vehicle design is evolving rapidly, and new, more efficient solutions to old problems are constantly challenging established and generalised assumptions. For instance, in vehicles built since the 1980s, other things being equal, the difference between front and rear drive in fuel economy terms is likely to be of little consequence.

The slightly modified, more aerodynamic, frontal treatment of this Volkswagen Polo Bluemotion helps improve fuel consumption, in turn, lowering exhaust emissions.

There now exist a number of alternatives to the petrol- and diesel-engined cars that have dominated motoring for so long. Hybrids are an obvious example, but practical electric cars, so-called 'dual fuel' LPG-powered cars, and vehicles capable of running on other alternative fuels are also available. These are discussed later, but for now we will look at the important aspects to consider when choosing diesel and petrol cars with both good fuel economy and the lowest possible emissions in mind.

Those government figures ...
A good place to start when choosing a new car is the manufacturers' published fuel consumption and emission figures. This data comes from standardised laboratory testing, undertaken during the type approval process before vehicles can legally be used on European roads. New car showrooms in Britain make this data available for vehicles currently on sale, but it's important to recognise such data is intended only for use in directly comparing the various vehicles offered by different makers in a static situation. Individual cars can (and do) achieve quite different figures – better or worse – in everyday real-world use. The showroom labelling system required by legislation indicates fuel consumption in three standard, so-called 'drive cycles,'

13

and includes a colour-coded chart indicating where that particular car falls in the various CO_2 emissions ratings. Since May 2009, these range from the most fuel efficient, band A (up to 100g/km), to the least efficient, band M (more than 255g/km). These bands relate directly to vehicle taxation levels, and are used to determine both the amount of annual road tax due, and the level of showroom tax, introduced from April 2010.

In general terms, the more fuel-efficient the car, the less vehicle excise duty and showroom tax will be payable. Even so, if you're buying a brand new car in Britain, it's wise to consider the recently introduced showroom tax – and the way it is applied – in some detail. This is because its banding structure has been set in a way that tends to penalise some small to medium size cars (and one or two larger ones) that might, until the tax introduction, have been considered reasonably economical, with relatively modest CO_2 emissions. For more information on the latest UK rules relating to vehicle taxation and current tax rates, visit www.directgov.uk/motoring.

The published information on drive cycles is derived from testing one example of any particular vehicle make and model under tightly controlled workshop conditions – no practical driving in the ever-varying conditions found on the road is involved. This approach is favoured because of the impossibility of guaranteeing consistency if each vehicle, from dozens of manufacturers, had to separately undergo real-world, on-road testing. The resulting data is thus useful for making direct model-to-model and brand-to-brand comparisons, and understanding the taxation costs involved – all while choosing a car in the showroom. Once the car is on the road, it's unlikely you'll get fuel consumption figures matching those in the published literature. Indeed, several drivers of the same car are very likely to get quite different results.

In thinking about driving to maximise economy, the combined economy figure is of most interest as a useful initial target to aim for in day-to-day driving. You might not come close, but equally, you might match or improve on it. The published figures are neither right nor wrong, they are simply an indication of what happens in a particular set of theoretical circumstances. On the road there are many variable factors affecting achievable fuel consumption, so unless there is a really significant variation, which might indicate a fault, how your

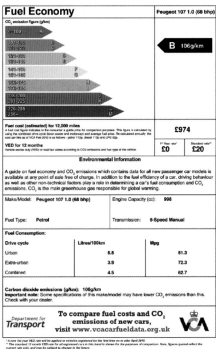

Helpful labels showing fuel consumption, taxation and emissions data are required on new cars displayed in British showrooms.

car shapes up in use compared to those official figures is not a great cause for concern. Use the paperwork to make a careful, informed choice about the best car for your situation, and then concentrate on making it stretch each drop of fuel as far as possible.

Making the best choice for you

The key fact an efficient driver needs to bear in mind when considering an eco-efficient car is that the carbon dioxide (CO_2) output of internal combustion engines relates directly to fuel type, and proportionately to fuel consumption.

If power outputs are similar, a typical diesel engine in a modern car will usually use less fuel and produce less CO_2 per mile than a petrol engine in the same model. However, various other exhaust pollutants are emitted in differing quantities by petrol and diesel engines, so here the rule remains: whatever the fuel, burn less of it overall, and you'll reduce emissions – of any sort – and hence create less pollution.

Modern engine and exhaust management systems work constantly to maximise fuel effiency and minimise pollutants, limiting environmental impact as far as the technology allows. Older cars inevitably have less effective systems, having been designed to meet the less stringent legislation that prevailed in the past. So, within limits (which we'll come to in a moment), to minimise environmental impact *and* get the best fuel economy, it's important to buy the newest car you can, preferably a current model, and then use economy-driving techniques whenever possible.

Small cars will always have a head start on fuel consumption, so it follows that if you want the very best economy (and minimum environmental impact) a small, light car will be your starting point. Yet though they are usually – but not universally – more economical than larger cars, small vehicles will not suit every driver's needs. If your circumstances require a bigger, heavier, or more powerful car, the distance travelled on each gallon of fuel will be less, and emissions will be higher. To offset this, cast aside prejudices and ask yourself some pointed questions. How big a car do I really, really need? Which fuel type will be best? Will a hybrid fit the bill? How many seats and how much loadspace is actually necessary? Do I genuinely need an automatic gearbox, the complexity of four-wheel-drive, the space of a big people carrier, or the largest capacity, highest performance engine?

For optimum economy choose a car with no sporting pretensions, without top-of-the-range luxury fittings and optional extras, and try to resist the temptation to use a trailer, or fit roof racks or roof boxes. These inevitably add weight or wind resistance, usually both, which increase fuel consumption. Convertible-type cars with a soft-top or foldaway hard-top should be avoided too when searching for best economy, as they are likely to be heavier (because of structural reinforcement or additional mechanical components) than equivalent size hardtop vehicles. Also, in the mass market at least, the aerodynamics of convertible or foldaway hard-top cars tend to be inferior to the standard versions from which they are usually developed. Though a foldaway hard-top roof might reasonably be expected to be more aerodynamically efficient than soft-top varieties, whatever the actual type, with the roof down, the vehicle's wind resistance will be significantly increased. This in turn will have a negative effect on fuel economy, especially when cruising top-down at higher speeds.

Foldaway hard-top cars like this Vauxhall Astra Twin Top can be more energy-efficient in the long-term than traditional soft-top convertibles. (Courtesy Vauxhall Motors)

Choosing a car with an automatic gearbox is likely to bring a fuel consumption penalty, simply because of the way most of these units operate. Nowadays there are several different kinds of gearboxes that can operate in automatic mode. Some newer automatics (introduced since 2000) can be almost as economical as their manual equivalents, and whatever type of gearbox is fitted, an economy-oriented driving style can certainly be adopted. Whilst there are some specialised tips to get the best out of an automatic car (see pages 36-37), many of the techniques described later for

manual vehicles can – at least in general – be applied to automatics, to show some economy benefits. Bear in mind, though, the improvements are likely to be much less pronounced.

Yet whatever vehicle you decide to run, be it a big car, an automatic, a people carrier, a sports model, or even a 4x4, by adopting a slightly different driving style, all can be persuaded to reduce the amount of fuel they consume. Vehicles like these are never likely to be best choice from a pure ecological standpoint, but this is a practical world, and any fuel consumption improvement does mean reduced emissions generally. Good fuel economy figures can be obtained from the most unlikely vehicles, and such achievements bring genuine driver satisfaction. With time and experience, there's no reason why you shouldn't stretch every gallon of fuel further – no matter what vehicle you drive.

Hybrid cars broadly follow the ground rules already mentioned: they are relatively low emitting, relatively economical vehicles, and are taxed accordingly – often at what some regard as preferential levels. For many years, the choice of hybrid passenger cars in Europe has been limited to a tiny handful of models, but this is set to become a growth area in future, because of perceived point of use ecological benefits. They also represent an attractive way for manufacturers to reduce average emissions values across a model range, which will become increasingly important in complying with future legislation. If running a hybrid appeals as an efficient way of getting around, the manufacturers' information will reveal immediate fuel consumption and emissions advantages compared to conventional cars of similar size and performance, particularly those with petrol engines. Maintenance and servicing costs should not be significantly higher, but this can, of course, be checked at the service reception desk of any dealership. The real questions may come with age, as failures in complex hybrid drivetrains and electronic systems – and heavy duty battery packs – could potentially give rise to significant expenditure if and when major parts require replacement.

Hybrid cars will respond to the economy driving techniques outlined in section 2 of this book, though any improvements gained may not be as marked as with more conventional vehicles.

Petrol or diesel?

When choosing a new car, deciding whether it should use petrol or diesel is vitally important. To arrive at a cost-effective decision, the efficient driver will find paper and a calculator helpful. Note your expected total annual mileage, and relate it to the vehicle's expected average fuel consumption, first with a petrol engine of the chosen power output, and then the equivalent diesel engine. In each case continue to calculate the total fuel cost for a year's motoring using appropriate or anticipated fuel prices.

If no clear cash benefit in favour of diesel is immediately revealed, a petrol version of the car is likely to be the optimum choice in your circumstances. However, even if some cash benefit in favour of diesel is apparent on mileage alone, it's possible a petrol engine could still emerge as the favoured option. Check with your local dealer or garage for the current total costs of routine, scheduled maintenance for both petrol and diesel variants over the period you intend to keep the car, and add this into your calculations. Often, model for model, petrol-fuelled cars will work out cheaper to maintain over a given period, particularly when covering up to 12,000 miles a year. If there's still a clear financial benefit over the petrol costings, or the calculations are very close, go with the diesel car.

The acknowledged longevity of diesel engines offsets these calculations. If you are intending to run a car for hundreds of thousands of miles, a diesel engine would most often be the reasonable choice because of its inherent ability to cover very significant mileages, as well as its generally better fuel economy. Over long distances, running costs will be proportionately lower, and the car's depreciation will become negligible as age and mileage build. The diesel vehicle will also deliver significant CO_2 emission benefits compared to an equivalent petrol engine over very high mileages.

Whilst diesel always appears tempting in comparisons of otherwise similar cars because of its better headline economy potential, it's important not to get carried away by this advantage in isolation. For many drivers covering less than 12,000 miles a year, if fuel prices are equal or diesel more expensive, petrol is likely to prove the wiser choice from an overall running cost point of view.

There is, though, another important aspect worth considering. Vehicle size, type, and performance are all clearly important in relation to fuel economy, but they are also important in relation to exhaust emissions. It's useful to be aware of the prevailing European legislative standards, which have been in place for some years and are gradually being tightened to further restrict vehicle pollution. The 2008 European emissions standard for cars was known as Euro IV, with Euro V enacted during 2009, one of the principal effects of which was to reduce the permitted particulate matter emissions from diesel cars from 25 milligrams per kilometre (mg/km) to 5mg/km. The even more challenging Euro VI, due in January 2014, will see the permitted emissions of nitrogen oxide from diesel cars reduced from 180mg/km to 80mg/km.

Because these standards are becoming more onerous over a long period, outwardly identical vehicles registered at different times may have some mechanical differences, since during their production lifetime they may have been required to meet different standards (e.g. Euro III and Euro IV). As a result, their fuel economy and exhaust emissions performance can be

different, sometimes in a swings-and-roundabouts situation which may lead to a trade-off between cleaner exhaust and slightly higher fuel consumption.

Whatever its type or size, or the fuel it uses, once settled on a vehicle, bear in mind that if you make a long-term commitment to adopt economy driving techniques, size for size and performance for performance, petrol or diesel, today's cars in general are capable of much better fuel consumption figures and lower emissions than the cars of the past. Buy the newest vehicle you can afford to obtain the best combination of ecological and economy benefits, both of which result from the most recent design thinking.

The 4x4 dilemma
If the chunky looks, interior space, commanding seating position, and towing or off-road ability of a traditional four-wheel-drive or Sport Utility Vehicle (SUV) appeal, be prepared to take a hit on vehicle excise duty, and if it's run as a company car, on taxation as well. Expect also to pay a penalty in exhaust emissions, fuel consumption, and general running costs, no matter what economy driving techniques you practice. All things are relative, and 4x4 vehicles come in a wide range of styles and sizes, ranging from genuine workhorses with few frills to those with high levels of performance and luxury equipment. All, however, are subservient to the laws of physics, which ensures at least some – possibly a large – negative impact in emissions and economy when compared to 'ordinary' cars of a similar size or performance class.

As a generic breed, 4x4s and SUVs have had a pretty consistently bad press since the activities of various vocal pressure groups convinced some sectors of the media and

Smaller versions of this vast, US market Cadillac Escalade have been offered in Britain, featuring a 6.2-litre petrol engine, 383g/km CO_2 emissions, and 17.4mpg combined fuel consumption. (Courtesy General Motors)

general public they automatically carry awesome ecological penalties. Much negative publicity sprang from selectively released research conducted on American SUVs, which are almost invariably much larger and much heavier than the vast majority of those found in Britain and Europe, and mostly powered by petrol engines of formidable capacity. Some American SUVs have much more in common with small European trucks in their basic design approach, and they usually feature big, powerful engines, lazy automatic gearboxes, and barn-door aerodynamics. A few have crossed the Atlantic, and even a cursory glance will reveal such vehicles are bigger than normal European expectations for an SUV, a difference that can also extend to notably higher fuel consumption and emissions. It's pretty unreasonable to regard such vehicles as mechanically comparable to the vast majority of SUVs found in Europe.

It follows that the emissions and fuel consumption penalties of European SUVs are not necessarily as severe as the scaremongers make out – though the omens are still far from good. Anyone searching for lowest emissions and best fuel economy would be well advised to entirely exclude from their research 4x4s as a breed. The reasons for this are quite straightforward. By definition, because of a 'dual purpose' ability, four-wheel-drive vehicles contain more complex drivetrains, usually offer poorer aerodynamics, and have greater weight. They also often have vastly bigger tyres, permanent all-wheel-drive with accompanying extra drag, and higher capacity, more powerful engines than an 'ordinary' car with equivalent or better roadgoing performance.

Several makers offer Sport Utility Vehicles with a choice of two- or four-wheel-drive transmission. The Kia Sportage variants shown here appear outwardly identical.

SUVs nonetheless come in a range of sizes, and various manufacturers have pointed out that some versions of their most recent road-oriented 4x4s are not significantly worse in government fuel consumption tests (and occasionally even better) than some 'ordinary' cars of equivalent size. Indeed, a few makers offer models that maintain the style, seating position, and ground clearance of near-identical 4x4 versions, but utilise only two-wheel-drive, benefiting economy and emissions.

Whatever the actual vehicle, reduced mechanical complexity is likely to help optimise fuel economy and minimise both emissions and long-term running costs. Real world use of four-wheel-drive vehicles may well show inferior fuel economy compared to two-wheel-drive versions, but bear in mind that, by virtue of other, separate factors

such as weight, aerodynamics, overall gearing, and rolling resistance, the two-wheel-drive version is still very likely to prove noticeably less economical overall than a similarly sized, similarly powerful, 'ordinary' car.

In the context of differences measured over days, weeks, or even months, we are really discussing shades of grey. But over the mileages associated with a period of ownership of three or more years, in economy and emissions terms the odds are stacked against SUV and 4x4 vehicles – and more heavily stacked the larger, heavier, and more complex they are. If you are looking for the most economical and efficient way of getting around, an SUV or larger four-wheel-drive vehicle is unlikely to be the answer.

If such a vehicle is necessary, first narrow down the possibilities to no more than two or three of the most compact, modestly specified, manual transmission vehicles that will meet your needs. Then closely study the relevant manufacturer's information for each of these vehicles. In addition to the usual economy and emissions figures, look particularly for any special, built-in, eco-related features. If the vehicle comes with selectable four-wheel-drive, normal running in two-wheel-drive mode is preferable, and can help economy (and reduce tyre wear) if most mileage is covered on metalled surfaces. Other things to look for include innovations such as engine stop-start, the lightest possible vehicle weight, the narrowest possible wheels and tyres, and any available aerodynamic information, often shown as a 'Cd' figure. Most practical modern cars currently return Cd figures in the range of 0.3 to 0.4, with lower numbers indicating reduced aerodynamic drag. Because of their big wheels, high ground clearance, and traditionally chunky, upright nature, SUVs, and bigger 4x4s generally, will rarely win prizes for efficient aerodynamics. Nonetheless, choosing an SUV with the lowest possible Cd figure may deliver some useful accumulated economy benefits over a lengthy ownership period, particularly if significant mileage is likely to be covered at higher speeds.

Technical stuff

For most drivers today, the under-bonnet workings of their vehicle are likely to be a closed book. Aside from carrying out the various regular checks suggested in vehicle handbooks – such as oil, water, and windscreen washer fluid levels and tyre pressures – given skilled attention at specified maintenance intervals, modern vehicle reliability is such that there is little need to know precisely what happens under the bonnet. However, there are a few areas where legislation or technological advances have a particular impact on vehicle efficiency, emissions, or fuel consumption, and these are outlined in this section.

If you are not of a technical frame of mind, there's no need to worry – you can safely skip to chapter 2 at this point, to discover how to drive more economically and efficiently.

Diesel particulate filters – their importance and their workings

For a given engine size and power output, modern diesel engines will in general produce both better fuel economy and emit less greenhouse gas than petrol units, although both fuel types still deliver other undesirable by-products into the atmosphere. In particular, diesels have become notorious for the health related issues surrounding so-called 'particulate matter' (PM) emissions.

Individual manufacturers are addressing this according to their view of the best way forward for their own vehicles, but the usual solutions involve fitting 'particulate traps' or 'diesel particulate filters' (DPFs). As their names imply, these are on-board systems that filter out much of the ecologically controversial particulate content in diesel exhaust. However, if left unattended, any filter could eventually become blocked, which could have serious consequences in a vehicle exhaust system. Arrangements are thus made in vehicle DPF systems to prevent such gradual blockage. In simpler systems, this may involve manual filter cleaning during routine servicing, usually at intervals of 50 to 70 thousand miles.

The actual DPF type used depends on the amount and size of particulates that must be removed. The simpler 'oxidation catalyst' and filter is known as a passive system. In this, particulates are burnt off using nitrogen dioxide from the exhaust stream passing through the catalyst. This process is known as regeneration, and takes place at around 250-450 degrees C, temperatures typically found in diesel exhausts. Such systems can trap perhaps 50 to 60 per cent of particulate matter, with the important bonus from a design, cost, and fuel efficiency standpoint being that no special external controls or additional energy input are required. Passive regeneration can take place continuously whenever the engine is delivering a good percentage of its power, and is most effective when travelling at motorway speeds. Whilst overall there may be some very slight fuel economy penalty resulting from a passive DPF fitment, there is nothing specific the economy-oriented driver can do to offset this.

As we move into and beyond the application of Euro V emissions standards, 'active' DPF regeneration is becoming increasingly unavoidable, due to the volume and gradually reducing size of the particulate matter to be dealt with. Again, the exact vehicle system and its operation (and the periods between any workshop attention) will vary among manufacturers. Some systems require periodic maintenance involving filter cleaning, and yet others the use of an additive that may need replenishment at infrequent intervals. The general outline of operation is as follows.

Active regeneration usually requires the temperature of the filter used to be above 550 degrees C, whereupon its contents will burn rapidly in oxygen (of which there is a plentiful supply in diesel exhaust gas). Depending on the vehicle use and prevailing engine conditions, a controlled additional hydrocarbon content – usually an amount of extra fuel – may be added at intervals to the exhaust, where it can be burnt to raise the filter temperature high enough for the process to take place effectively. This requirement is detected, and the cycle involved precisely controlled, by the engine management system.

Whilst active DPF regeneration is thus vital from emission control and exhaust system reliability standpoints, it also has a slight but unavoidable negative impact for drivers concerned about optimum fuel economy. This is because, in many cases, the DPF temperature is raised by electronically adjusting the quantity of fuel burnt by the engine, the precise time in the engine's cycle when the fuel is injected, or even by injecting fuel into the exhaust system, where it plays no useful part in propelling the car. In terms of vehicle efficiency and fuel economy none of this is encouraging, as although it is not a large amount, any fuel leaving the engine unburnt, or inadequately burnt, or indeed fed into the exhaust system, is, in straightforward economy terms, wasted.

Whilst it may seem reasonable to demand that lower particulate emissions are not achieved through such a reduction in fuel efficiency, at the current state of DPF development this is really unavoidable, since some energy beyond that needed to move the vehicle is necessary to deliver the desired effect in the DPF. Extra fuel is thus required to ensure the vehicle delivers the lower emissions demanded by legislation.

Fortunately, in an economy context, this active regeneration process may take place quite infrequently, since its occurrence depends largely on the conditions under which the vehicle is used. As we shall see later, conditions under which active DPF regeneration is most likely to be prompted also happen to be those which the efficient driver will seek to avoid as far as possible. As a result, though the process will still inevitably take place from time to time, its penalty on overall fuel economy is at least to some extent mitigated.

The frequency of the active DPF regeneration cycle is minimised when a vehicle is predominantly used away from urban and low speed conditions, in situations where speeds are generally above 50 miles an hour – preferably including a good proportion of faster motorway work. If the car is used for significant lengths of time at lower speeds and light engine loads – say in urban driving -–the active DPF regeneration system is likely to operate more frequently, typically perhaps every 500 or 600 miles driven, even if this includes a proportion of higher speed work.

A complete operational cycle can take up to 3 or 4 minutes, during which time a slight performance loss and some increase in exhaust smoke may be noticed. Under some low-speed traffic conditions where an active regeneration cycle has been initiated, it's possible that a dashboard warning light may illuminate to indicate the process has not been successful. Some systems utilise warning lights to indicate a range of problems, including low additive levels, which require periodic top up. Consult the vehicle handbook for specific advice if such

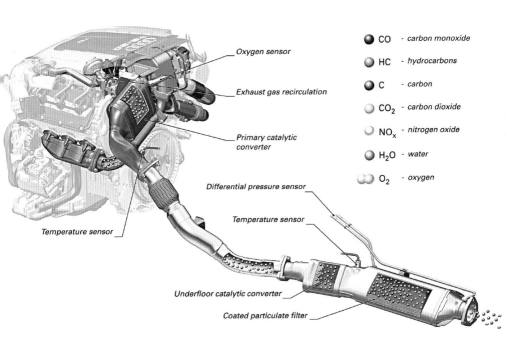

Oxygen sensor

Exhaust gas recirculation

Primary catalytic converter

Differential pressure sensor

Temperature sensor

Temperature sensor

Underfloor catalytic converter

Coated particulate filter

Temperature sensor

CO - carbon monoxide

HC - hydrocarbons

C - carbon

CO_2 - carbon dioxide

NO_x - nitrogen oxide

H_2O - water

O_2 - oxygen

A DPF system layout, as fitted to some Audi A4s. The 'differential pressure sensor' allows detection of declining filter performance, enabling regeneration to be initiated. (Courtesy Audi UK)

warning lights appear. In some cases, it may well be possible for a vehicle user to clear problems through such things as additive replenishment or a high-speed run (say above 45mph). However, if this proves not to be the case, and warning lights remain on, a dealer for the make of car should be consulted without delay, as damage may result – and replacement DPFs are expensive ...

'Clean diesel' technology – for cars of the future

Responding to Euro VI emission requirements due to come into force in 2014, car manufacturers are currently developing methods to reduce nitrogen oxide (NOx) emissions – a distinctly unwanted by-product of the combustion process in diesel engines. From a pollution standpoint, the long-term suppression of NOx from vehicle exhausts is regarded by some experts as being as crucial as the progress made in steadily reducing vehicle CO_2 emissions in recent years. Nitrogen oxide is a particularly undesirable atmospheric pollutant because of its links to known health risks – if left unchecked, on contact with sunlight it may form photochemical smog, a type of pollution that can cause lung tissue damage. It is also a key component in the formation of both acid rain and ground level ozone.

A few manufacturers have already announced vehicles able to meet the 2014 requirements, and more will follow as the Euro VI deadline draws nearer. For example, some variants of the 2010 model year Audi Q7 offered in Britain feature what the company describes as its 'clean diesel' system. This is said to be capable of removing up to 90 per cent of nitrogen oxide from the exhaust gas, allowing early compliance with the expected emission limits.

This technology operates using a highly efficient and carefully controlled combustion process, after which engine exhaust gases are routed via a special NOx-trap catalytic converter built into the exhaust system. Here, a pump injects a part-urea, part de-ionised water solution into the exhaust flow, where it decomposes into ammonia. In turn, this splits potentially harmful nitrogen oxide into inert nitrogen gas, oxygen and water.

In Europe, the solution used in such systems is commonly known either as automotive urea solution (AUS), or by its registered trade name of Adblue. This has the formal title of 'reagent AUS32' – a reagent being a substance used to initiate a chemical reaction. It has been used for some time in systems called selective catalytic reducers (SCRs) to reduce NOx emissions from larger commercial vehicles, buses and coaches. Here, it's often used in a proportion of up to 5 per cent of the diesel fuel tank capacity – though at no stage is it actually mixed with the fuel. On larger vehicles, covering long distances with significant fuel consumption, for convenience the additive is frequently carried in tanks filled by the driver from an appropriate pump, in a similar way to the fuel itself – albeit in modest quantities.

However, smaller vehicles require much less additive to achieve useful results. Using the Audi Q7 SUV as an example, its 3.0-litre diesel engine can be specified with clean diesel technology at an additional cost (at launch) of £1500 over standard versions. The car then includes a 23-litre AUS tank, from which additive is consumed in a variable amount of 0.5 to 1 per cent of fuel quantity. The tank would thus be emptied at intervals equating to consumption of not less than 2300 litres of diesel fuel, which, using the vehicle's 31.7mpg government combined consumption figure as a guide, suggests it could travel at least 16,000 miles – and possibly beyond 30,000 miles – between additive refills. Servicing of this vehicle is required at either fixed intervals of 10,000 miles, or at variable intervals determined through vehicle usage by the on-board computer system. Either way, remembering

to replenish the additive should not concern drivers – it's included in the routine workshop service schedule. However, as a safeguard, a dashboard warning light system is also fitted, counting down time until replenishment is needed. Other manufacturers use different methods – for example, the latest versions of the Mazda CX7 have a miniature AUS gauge built into the main dashboard fuel gauge.

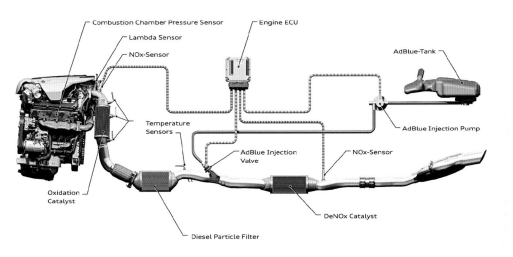

An outline of Audi's 'clean diesel' system. More vehicles will include such systems, as the implementation date for Euro 6 emissions standards draws closer.
(Courtesy Audi UK)

two

Driving for maximum efficiency

How to drive economically – and finding out how your search for economy is going

Before starting out, please remember: in developing your skills to drive more economically, the first priority must remain the safety of yourself, your passengers and other road users. Always be ready to adapt to ever-changing traffic conditions, and be prepared at any time to switch away from economy driving techniques to an alternative style more suited to the new conditions.

Don't hesitate to temporarily sacrifice fuel economy in the interests of road safety if it becomes necessary for any reason. There'll be plenty more opportunities to practice your economical driving skills.

The basics ...

Improved fuel economy doesn't happen by accident – it involves making use of plenty of inside knowledge and general driving experience, and great attention to detail. Many factors can influence fuel economy, and some of them are not immediately obvious. They include vehicle size, weight, ground clearance and aerodynamics, fuel type, engine design, power output, overall gearing, tyre type and construction, the legislative rules applying when the car was designed, the way it's loaded, how well and how frequently it's serviced, the weather, the current traffic situation, the amount of electrical equipment in use – even the car's present height above sea level.

Some of these we can do very little about, but there is one key component not mentioned so far, one that has considerably more long-term impact on fuel economy than any other – the driver. Over time, it is the way a vehicle in good working order is used that has the most significant effect on fuel consumption, and that's something for which the driver alone has direct responsibility.

Economy driving techniques are often perceived by members of the 'press-on-regardless' brigade as invariably requiring progress at a snail's pace, creating traffic hold-ups at every turn and frustration among other road users. You may well have noticed – though such critics probably haven't – that there are already plenty of drivers out there doing just that, and they really don't appear to be doing it in pursuit of the best possible fuel economy.

The fact is, critics tarring those striving to improve fuel economy (and lower exhaust emissions) with the same brush as thoughtless and inconsiderate drivers will know little and care less about the finesse or satisfaction involved in skilful driving – of which economy driving is a close relation. It follows they'll also know little about how better fuel economy is really achieved. They probably don't pay for the fuel they use, or the maintenance of the vehicle on which they put unnecessary pressure. These are drivers who will almost certainly break the law and cause plenty of frustration themselves as they routinely make a habit out of being genuinely bad drivers, with little regard for the consequences of their inadequate observation and ill-considered actions on other road users. As you start to practice economy driving techniques, you'll see plenty of them. Don't be put off by uninformed critics.

With practice, by appreciating, developing and applying the skills of logic, observation, mirror use, anticipation and car control, it's perfectly possible to drive economically, within the law, in town or out, at or around the speed of other traffic, performing safe and swift overtaking when needed, making useful progress without getting in anyone else's way.

Having said that, safe driving on today's crowded roads can never involve being mindlessly eco-exclusive. There will inevitably be times when it becomes necessary to drive to minimise congestion, and plenty more when firm acceleration or braking is the right – and probably the only correct – action for the circumstances. Balanced over a period of time, such things will not have a hugely significant impact on your overall fuel consumption figure. Eco-driving involves a definite learning curve, plus an empathy with, and understanding of, how your vehicle can make the most efficient progress. Though eco-driving is far more about brain-power than horsepower, it's always worth bearing in mind that use of one does not automatically exclude use of the other.

Planning ...

It might seem obvious, but one very good way to cut fuel consumption is not to use the car at all, or minimise its use as far as possible. If you have a regular weekday school run or commute to work, try and share a car. Make arrangements to team up with friends or colleagues making similar regular journeys, and rotate car use amongst the group. This allows the costs of making each trip to be split, while easing parking worries and reducing pollution and congestion at the same time. Various websites have sprung up offering to match those making similar journeys every day, and who therefore may be able to car share. Many county councils and unitary authorities participate in and encourage such schemes – check your local authority's website to see if a system

Regular commuting can be made more eco-efficient through a car share arrangement.
Various local authorities promote schemes online and by telephone, via these roadside signs.

is operating in your area. The website www.liftshare.com may also be of help.

If you need to make a short journey, try very hard not to make it by car – walk, cycle, or take a bus instead. Quite apart from saving fuel, a little exercise could also help to improve your health. Vehicle engines consume proportionately more fuel in the immediate aftermath of a cold start, and things hardly improve if what follows is a short, stop and start journey of a mile or two. In general, if average speeds are low, congestion rife, and the distance covered relatively short, all the elements conducive to the worst possible fuel economy are neatly combined. Making such a journey with a cold engine as well is just compounding matters. Such journeys usually involve noticeable amounts of time with the engine idling; it's always worth bearing in mind that an engine that is running without moving the car is achieving a particularly noteworthy economy figure – zero miles per gallon.

If using a car in urban or congested conditions cannot realistically be avoided, use forward planning to negate the impact, not just on fuel economy, but also on emissions and congestion. All could be favourably influenced by combining journeys, planning an efficient route using readily available traffic information, and travelling outside peak hours. If yours is a two-car family, get into the habit of considering the most ecologically-appropriate vehicle for each journey – not the bigger-engined car for a trip to the shops simply because it's 'yours.' Instead of driving from home to the supermarket at 5 o'clock today, and from home to the DIY store at 9 o'clock tomorrow morning, if possible try combining those journeys at 2.30 in the afternoon, using a carefully planned route to avoid likely delays. The total mileage on such a circular trip might be slightly more, but offsetting that are reduced congestion delays, less chance of lengthy waits at, say, temporary traffic lights, and the engine will have had only one cold start plus time to reach its proper operating temperature, making it more efficient for most of the journey.

When undertaking any journey, try not to get lost. Avoid driving round a town looking for an address or parking area. Plan the route in advance using satellite navigation (see pages 57-58), town centre plans, or street maps readily available on the internet. Don't forget to take account of one-way streets. If you're undertaking a long journey, take time beforehand to plan your route with a road atlas. Look for the line of least resistance in choosing the roads to use – motorways and dual carriageways with minimised gradients usually offer the best conditions for smooth, eco-friendly travel, but they do suffer from congestion at certain times, which could markedly reduce overall fuel economy on your route. Try to plan for travel at an eco-friendly time, when traffic is at lower levels, remembering that delays and congestion always mean increased overall fuel consumption and exhaust emissions.

Consider a slightly longer route overall if your journey will take you up hill and down dale along single carriageway roads – or through numerous towns and villages: another few miles of motorway or dual carriageway cruising are preferable in economy terms to a route a few miles shorter but involving steep hills and lots of slower moving traffic. Allow enough time, so that there is no need to drive at the 70mph speed limit for hours on end. Cruising at 70mph,

you could be using up to 25 per cent more fuel than at 50mph, and reducing cruising speed by just 10mph could help improve fuel economy by several mpg. Even slight speed reductions can save a worthwhile amount of fuel on longer journeys.

For safety's sake, build some rest periods of at least half an hour into journeys exceeding a couple of hours.

Starting ...
Whatever the journey to be undertaken, remember to avoid starting the engine if you're not driving away immediately – and don't pump the throttle at any stage, it will just waste fuel. Today's engine management systems have removed any valid reason for 'warming up' before driving off, and are well capable of accurately optimising the precise amount of fuel needed for the easiest possible start, no matter what the prevailing weather conditions when you turn that key.

Note, however, that unless a manufacturer has installed extra equipment, once under way diesel engines may take noticeably longer than petrol units to warm up. This is because they are more thermodynamically efficient – that is, better than petrol engines at turning fuel into movement of the engine itself, and ultimately the vehicle. Less fuel is thus wasted generating unwanted heat, so the engine warms up comparatively slowly. This can be particularly noticeable in winter months, when the heater may take time to have an impact. The downside here is that diesel fuel consumption can be poorer in the few miles after a completely cold start, because the engine does not reach optimum working temperature very quickly. It's another good reason not to use the car on relatively short journeys, especially in winter.

Thoughtless parking inconveniences pedestrians, and wastes fuel. Avoid blocking pavements when parking, and remember the fuel economy benefits of exiting parking spaces forwards. (Courtesy Reg Burnard)

Always reverse into your driveway or garage, thus minimising 'cold' manoeuvring when next starting, because you can then drive out forwards. Next time you need the car, try to just start and go, departing as soon as traffic allows, with as little engine idling as possible. When manoeuvring into or out of parking spaces at any time, don't needlessly slip the clutch and rev the engine – be gentle, and keep the engine as near idling speed as is sensible. You may be 'just parking,' but the overriding aim should still be the avoidance of wasted fuel, with the bonus of reducing premature wear on the car's clutch components by tiptoe-ing into and out of parking spaces. Try also to be courteous to pedestrians; don't

encroach on the pavement with a parked vehicle, blocking their way. Life's difficult enough for the blind or partially sighted, and mums with prams and pushchairs!

In cold weather, get up earlier, have suitable screen clearing equipment available, and use it before you start and go. On the move, don't be frightened to use the defrosting systems to rapidly clear the glass and external mirrors. In winter, remember it's an offence to drive a vehicle with partially obscured vision in any direction. Make sure all the glass is cleared before starting.

Here's another key to saving money through fuel economy: always invest in some intelligent thinking before setting out, and try not to drive unless you really have to.

Speed Limits

Type of vehicle	Built-up areas* mph (km/h)	Single carriage-ways mph (km/h)	Dual carriage-ways mph (km/h)	Motorways mph (km/h)
Cars & motorcycles (including car-derived vans up to 2 tonnes maximum laden weight)	**30** (48)	**60** (96)	**70** (112)	**70** (112)
 **Cars towing caravans or trailers** (including car-derived vans and motorcycles)	**30** (48)	**50** (80)	**60** (96)	**60** (96)
 **Buses, coaches and minibuses** (not exceeding 12 metres in overall length)	**30** (48)	**50** (80)	**60** (96)	**70** (112)
Goods vehicles (not exceeding 7.5 tonnes maximum laden weight)	**30** (48)	**50** (80)	**60** (96)	**70**[†] (112)
 **Goods vehicles** (exceeding 7.5 tonnes maximum laden weight)	**30** (48)	**40** (64)	**50** (80)	**60** (96)

*The 30 mph limit usually applies to all traffic on all roads with street lighting unless signs show otherwise
[†] 60 mph (96 km/h) if articulated or towing a trailer.

For best fuel economy, know the speed limits that apply to your particular vehicle, and stay within them at all times. These are for the UK. (Reproduced under terms of a Click-Use Licence from the official Highway Code, revised 2007 edition)

On the move ...

One golden rule: obey speed limits the whole time. Britain, for instance, has a surprising range of speed limits, dependent on the type of road, the type of vehicle, and whether or not the vehicle is towing a trailer. Make sure you know the speed limits applicable to your vehicle – and don't break them.

Faster driving uses noticeably more fuel, so staying within speed limits will bring you immediate fuel economy improvements, and naturally reduces the risk of collecting speeding tickets to zero.

Your powers of observation and anticipation will also develop, as obeying speed limits involves looking further ahead to spot them and stay within them as they change.

Stopping (as little as you can ...)

Naturally, brakes must be used when needed, but they have a significant impact on fuel economy. Use the brakes less, and you'll use less fuel. Yes, really!

Here's why: keep in mind that, for manual transmission vehicles, with only limited exceptions (usually relating to travelling downhill and emergency situations), any speed you need to lose through brake use probably means that somewhere, just a little earlier, you accelerated the car slightly harder than strictly necessary. Fuel was thus consumed reaching a speed *beyond* that actually required for the conditions, and that fuel has been wasted, because it's now warming up the brakes when it could have been used for further powering the car. Using good anticipation to avoid needless braking thus means your overall fuel economy figure will improve. This said, repeatedly judging the precise amount of acceleration needed for any given traffic conditions is a very fine art indeed, requiring endless practice, but even

slightly reducing brake use will make a difference. Over-using the brakes is so common, this really rates as a core economy-driving issue.

This is all well and good at lower speeds, but on faster roads it's often very difficult indeed to judge conditions so as to avoid obstructing other traffic while reducing speed to negotiate a bend or slip road exit – all without braking. Bear in mind, too, that at main road and motorway speeds, other drivers come to rely on seeing brake lights ahead to plan their actions and take account of developing situations. If they don't see brake lights on your car, they might think you're not slowing down. Use rear view mirrors frequently to judge the changing situation behind in such cases, and don't risk a rear-end collision through dogmatically avoiding brake use.

Such situations can be an opportunity to develop the art of minimised braking, which will still ensure operation of brake lights for other road users' benefit. When approaching a bend or junction, or immediately before an exit slip road, come off the power as soon as reasonable given the traffic around you, and let the car lose speed by rolling in gear. Where slowing is necessary, call upon your developing powers of anticipation – make an early change from 6th to 5th, or 5th to 4th, allowing speed to decline smoothly. Use the brakes lightly, but as necessary, aiming to arrive at the hazard at a speed suitable for the manoeuvre you must make, with just sufficient momentum to allow appropriate gear selection for acceleration once your view is clear, OR a stop – still using minimal braking. Lots of practice will be needed, but it's a satisfying achievement, and it's still to the benefit of your fuel economy ...

Whatever the speed and conditions, the object for best economy must be to minimise brake use where it's safe, possible and fully realistic – NOT to avoid braking at any cost. Saving fuel and reducing emissions is important, but road safety is paramount, and the brakes should be used as hard as needed without hesitation. We all misjudge situations from time to time, and the driver must ALWAYS remain in full control... Don't hesitate – use the brakes!

Anticipating ...

As you'll quickly discover, staying off the brakes in today's traffic conditions is far from easy. However, driving inside speed limits with reduced brake usage constantly in mind is likely to mean you'll be travelling more slowly than usual, with important benefits to both fuel economy and road safety. Work towards your target of minimal braking by applying yourself wholeheartedly to the job in hand. Avoid distractions like the radio, and keep forcing yourself to constantly look further ahead. Pull back to allow a noticeable gap to the vehicle ahead, and consciously position your car for best forward visibility, continuously analysing the unfolding traffic situation around you and anticipating what will happen next, and how you can avoid hard braking when it does. Use your mirrors far more frequently. Become more fully aware of what's going on around you. Plan your moves before making them. Look in all the mirrors *before* you touch the indicator stalk, not as you touch it. Teach yourself to avoid driving faster than you can think. Mastering these skills will allow you to develop an altogether smoother driving technique, not just in town, but on all types of road.

On motorways, start looking further ahead, make more frequent use of mirrors, and discover also how slightly modulating your chosen cruising speed in good time, through early and gentle accelerator pedal use, can close or

These two vehicles are 88 feet (13.41 metres) apart – the minimum gap necessary to comply with the 'two-second rule' when travelling at 30mph.

increase the gap on the vehicle in front or behind. Developing this useful skill will allow you to slot into the adjacent lane for overtaking without needing to brake, and without obstructing faster traffic. Put the experience gained here to good use on single carriageway roads – leave plenty of room between you and the vehicle ahead, anticipate junctions, bends, roundabouts, and so on, and make speed adjustments early by observing and then responding to changing conditions so that, overall, less braking is necessary. In town, early speed adjustments will give more time for lights to change and traffic to clear, allowing you to progress smoothly, without hard (or any) braking.

Too close, too fast ...?

Close following compromises safety, and is the enemy of economical driving. It makes frequent brake use inevitable, and it seriously restricts visibility, leaving the following driver with few clues about what the driver ahead might do, or why. The smaller the gap to the vehicle ahead, the less room available to soak up the constant minor speed changes that occur in any traffic stream ... unless you use the brakes frequently, and you know what that does to fuel economy. At 30mph, you're covering 44 feet (13.41 metres) every second. Without an adequate gap, if the vehicle in front reduces speed even slightly, you'll be too close inside half a second, and what previously seemed a reasonable gap will instantly be halved. Instinct says reach for the brake – quick! That's more wasted fuel. Try hard to maintain the 'two-second rule' – that's 88 feet (26.82 metres) to the car ahead in town traffic, and just over 200 feet (60.96 metres) at 70mph.

Why get too close? Dropping back means you'll see more of what's happening ahead, gaining valuable time to react, and lessening the chances of having to brake. Time might be

These vehicles are 204 feet (60.96 metres) apart – two seconds at 70mph. At this speed, if the numberplate ahead is readable, you're getting too close!

pressing, but close following doesn't gain time; it worries the driver ahead, it's no way to start an overtake, and, most importantly, it prevents thoughtful response to traffic developments around you, reducing available time to rescue the situation if anything untoward occurs – and sooner or later, it will. Economical (and safe) drivers avoid close following like the plague.

The art of being gentle
Occasional, quite firm acceleration has less effect on overall fuel economy than you might think, but an important key to economical driving is always to use the accelerator delicately, with thoughtful precision. Imagine an egg underneath it – use it progressively, and don't break that egg through pressing the pedal over-enthusiastically. Avoid needlessly revving the engine, 'blipping' the throttle between gear changes, and hard acceleration away from traffic lights. Use the accelerator pedal as sparingly as possible, remembering that, if you're in traffic, racing between hold-ups at traffic lights, roundabouts, or road humps won't get you home noticeably quicker, but you'll be using the brakes quite a lot. Progress like that doesn't save any useful time, but will inevitably waste fuel.

Instead look for a comfortable balance. Use your right foot to minimise the peaks and troughs of acceleration and braking, while making reasonable progress given the state of the traffic, without needlessly holding up other drivers by being a slowcoach. Use the accelerator to get you to the next anticipated hazard smoothly but not too quickly, in the hope that it will be gone by the time you get there, so you can start planning how best to deal with the next problem. If you can, build up speed a little on downhill slopes to help carry you up the next gradient without adding great amounts of power – and when

cresting a rise, ease off the power just before reaching the summit, allowing vehicle momentum to take you the rest of the way and over the top. That's a little more fuel saved!

Though not really its primary purpose, a tachometer (rev counter) can help you drive more economically. Subject to such things as vehicle load, traffic and the gradient at the time, 2000 revs is an easily memorised general change-up point suiting many diesel cars in give-and-take motoring. Half the marked rev limit is an equivalent guide point for petrol engines, typically no higher than around 2500-3000 revs. Diesel engines will often work uncomplainingly down to very low revs, but it's important to try and develop a sympathetic ear: whatever the fuel, labouring an engine does nothing for either economy or mechanical longevity. Change down if things begin to get lumpy, or the vibes are telling you that the engine, transmission or driveline feels unhappy.

The right gear – at the right time ...
In general, high gears deliver best fuel economy, so use the highest gear possible as frequently as you can, but without labouring the engine at very low speeds. Look ahead for favourable conditions where it might be possible to move up through the gearbox, missing out gears that aren't really vital at that particular moment, especially when travelling downhill or on reaching your intended cruising speed on a level road. Many modern cars – particularly but not exclusively diesels – will happily move from second to fourth, or third to fifth. Downhill gradients with clear visibility often permit such 'block changes,' allowing a car to smoothly gather speed with a very modest throttle setting, minimising fuel used in the acceleration process.

Use favourable road layouts to your advantage – open downhill stretches like this allow early shifts to higher gears, providing best economy with little fuss.

Automatic considerations ...

Until the advent of increasingly sophisticated electronic control systems in the 1980s, automatic transmission cars could generally be relied upon to come with a noticeable fuel consumption penalty. Such transmissions were largely allied to big and often thirsty petrol engines, and at a time when fuel prices were comparatively low and environmental issues not a consideration, the increased fuel consumption was frequently accepted as 'just one of those things.' Since the 1990s automatic gearbox and control system design has moved forward dramatically, and various different types of automatic transmissions are now available, virtually all of which use some electronic control. The ubiquitous torque converter, basis of automatic setups for many years, is in decline, though it remains a cornerstone

of many larger automatic cars, albeit frequently with mechanical and electronic enhancements to improve driveability and fuel economy.

Continuously variable transmission (CVT) has become an important and more fuel-efficient alternative to automatics, mostly in cars below 2 litres, and there are now several different 'automated manual' gearboxes on the market, including Vauxhall's Easytronic, smart's softouch, and Peugeot/Citroën's Electronic Gearbox System (EGS) available in cars below 1.6 litres. Several versions of the Dynamic Shift Gearbox (DSG) pioneered by the VW Audi Group are making inroads at the mid and higher end of the market, being effectively two gearboxes in one, capable of good fuel economy and emissions performance through very rapid, almost imperceptible changes and reduced drivetrain power losses.

Some vehicles launched since 2009 by these manufacturers come with official CO_2 and fuel economy figures that are identical or slightly lower than their manual counterparts, though individual driving style will inevitably be a major factor in determining precisely how economical such vehicles prove on the road.

Some manufacturers nowadays claim that their current automatic gearboxes – most often the automated manual and DSG types – are more economical, and occasionally lower

Manual shift arrangements for automatic gearboxes vary considerably: here, the lever is shifted left, then pushed forward for upchanges and backward for downchanges.

emitting, than the equivalent fully manual car with the same engine. Government figures in some cases do show slightly better results for these types of gearbox. Citroën, indeed, has claimed a 6 per cent improvement in consumption on some models fitted with its EGS system. However, as we've seen, government figures don't involve real world testing, and in give-and-take use on the road, experience suggests that whilst such systems are usually more economical than a traditional automatic gearbox, genuine long-term economy advantages compared to a manual car tend to be far less clear-cut than the figures indicate.

Yet that same experience has shown that, in general, great strides have been made in getting automatic cars to deliver better fuel economy in recent years, and work continues to refine control systems. If you want to drive an automatic with economy in mind, in general the best starting point will be the latest model from your chosen manufacturer, preferably with a diesel engine. CVT and automated manual gearboxes seem to have a fuel economy advantage both on paper and in real world driving, but bear in mind they tend to be fitted to smaller-engined and smaller, lighter cars anyway, giving them something of a head start.

If there is one aspect common to many automatic gearboxes – particularly, but not exclusively, those of the past – which is the bane of the economy-minded driver, it's a tendency for many such units to drop into a 'neutral drive' condition with engine idling whenever power is removed by the driver. With no natural engine braking, this can result in the car rolling forward a surprising distance afterwards, making it virtually impossible to avoid braking on most occasions. Neither fuel economy nor brake lining life benefit from this, but unless you opt for one of the more recent types of automatic, brake use in these circumstances is pretty inevitable. Some newer automatics are designed to more closely replicate manual gearbox characteristics by providing at least some engine braking when power is removed, or alternatively to drop down the box automatically one gear at a time as speed declines. Such systems offer the potential for easier overall control of speed, reducing reliance on brake use, and – in tandem with engine overrun fuel shut-off systems – helping improve fuel economy.

Automatic gearboxes do tend to come with an exhaust emissions penalty, which can range from very modest to quite significant. The worst offenders tend to be older designs with only three or four ratios, and a torque converter drive system with neither overdrive ratio nor lock-up facility. Such gearboxes can result in much higher levels of CO_2 emissions when compared to an otherwise identical car with a 5-speed manual gearbox. Though dependent on overall power output, amongst more modern designs of typical mid-size cars a penalty of 50g/km is not unknown, and even with some of the latest, more efficient automatic systems, emissions can be over 20g/km worse.

If you are considering an automatic car, it will pay to closely study the manufacturers' published literature for all those in which you are potentially interested, so that the balance between best fuel economy and lowest emissions can be explored in detail. Since driving as economically as possible reduces both fuel usage and emissions, it will also pay to get hold of specific road test reports, to discover what happens in real world driving of the cars on your shortlist, and how that compares to the manufacturers'

published information. Having studied as much published data as possible, visit the relevant showrooms and ask about the type of automatic fitted to the vehicles you're interested in.

Look for cars with six- or even seven-speed automatic transmissions – there are an increasing number of these. Such automatics tend to have a wide ratio set, which can efficiently cover most driving situations and help boost economy, particularly when cruising at higher speeds over long distances. A long-striding sixth or seventh ratio will lower engine revs at cruising speed, helping to benefit an automatic car's fuel economy. As an indication of progress in automatic transmission design, during 2009, Hyundai introduced a new 6-speed automatic gearbox for some models; it still employed a torque converter, but fitted in the big Grandeur saloon it was said to deliver a 2.5 per cent improvement in standing start acceleration times, and 11 per cent in overtaking performance, while being a remarkable 12 per cent more economical than the 5-speed unit which it replaced. It was also more compact, 12kg lighter – and used 62 fewer component parts!

Once you have reached a decision on the automatic car that's right for you, try to arrange a reasonably lengthy test drive before purchasing. This will allow you to detect any foibles of the transmission, which can then be related to the severity of what are likely to be unavoidable fuel consumption and emissions penalties.

Driving automatics economically
Most of the techniques described in this book relating to manual cars hold good for automatics in broad terms, though as we've seen, in some cases it will be difficult to effectively apply some techniques to certain types of automatic

gearboxes. Nonetheless, there are a few tips specific to automatic transmission in general that can help improve fuel economy.

All automatics come with a 'kickdown' facility, activated by flooring the accelerator pedal: it's a good idea to avoid use of this as far as possible within the constraints of proper attention to both road safety and emergency situations, since it will not only cause the transmission to change down rapidly but probably also deliver additional fuel to the engine. In a manual car under normal circumstances, the economical driver will rarely have use for full throttle. If a lower ratio is needed quickly with automatic transmission, it will be more economical to use the manual selector lever, followed by brief, firm acceleration if needed. If you're looking well ahead – an economical driving keynote – you might also want to ask yourself why a lower ratio was needed in such a hurry ...

Most automatics can be persuaded to change up quite early whilst gaining speed if accelerator pedal pressure is moderated during the process. Often this can be done with little significant effect on acceleration, but it will reduce engine speeds, helping long-term fuel economy. Try to learn the sort of road speeds and gradient conditions where the system is most willing to change up – develop a routine, where conditions allow, of minimising the throttle setting, rather than leaving things to the box's inbuilt change points. From there, make a point of using the lowest engine speed possible for the prevailing conditions by being gentle with the pedal. The reason: with the clutch engaged, a manual car always has a positive connection between engine and road wheels – as engine speed rises, road speed rises in a fixed relationship. Many automatics introduce 'slip' into this relationship,

particularly at lower speeds, and whenever it occurs, it becomes a source of fuel wastage. If slip is present, you'll see it on the rev counter when you press the accelerator, and it can be heard too; the engine will speed up, but road speed remains little altered. Always try hard to minimise slip.

Conversely, if a driver asks for lots of power, many auto boxes will drop two ratios in quick succession. A less aggressive demand (or a manual downchange) might result in a drop of only one gear, saving fuel.

Because there are many different types of automatic transmission in use these days, and they differ in their reactions to the situation described here, what follows can only be generalised advice. If in doubt, consult an authorised dealer for your make of car.

With automatic gearboxes, there is a great driver temptation to use their ability to prevent the car rolling backwards on a slope by applying a little power whilst waiting at traffic lights, junctions and roundabouts. Where traffic conditions allow, try to avoid this. The engine is being asked to deliver slightly more power to counteract a gradient than it would at normal idle speed. In turn that means the engine is consuming more fuel than it might – whilst the vehicle is stationary. That's zero mpg. If you're driving an automatic and need to stop, unless the wait is very short, optimising fuel economy means it's usually best to apply the handbrake. At night, it also avoids dazzling the driver behind with your stoplights.

If you really want to make the absolute best of the economy situation here, shift the transmission into neutral after applying the handbrake, and re-select drive just before moving off. Even on a level road, many types of auto transmission continue to absorb power from the engine when stationary – again, it's a slight engine load that optimum fuel economy could do without. However, bear in mind also that repeatedly making this shift will eventually lead to wear in the shift mechanism and possibly the gearbox; the cost of any necessary repairs could outweigh the amount of fuel saved! Note also that some manufacturers now supply transmissions that automatically shift into neutral at idle, for the reasons explained above.

If your car has an adaptive auto box, try to consistently use as gentle a driving technique as possible. The box will 'learn' your relaxed driving style and shift its change-point characteristics, tuning itself for early upshifts and maximum economy. If the gearbox is one of the now steadily decreasing number with an overdrive ratio that can be deselected via a switch, think of the overdrive in much the same way as fifth gear in a manual gearbox. If an ongoing driving situation is such that speeds are relatively low (say below 40mph) and the roads are twisty or hilly, there would be little chance of using a manual fifth gear. In these situations, overdrive when allied to an automatic gearbox is probably better left switched off, for reasons of both better fuel economy and better car control. Conversely, don't hesitate to allow the overdrive system to operate whenever a manual box would be comfortable in holding fifth gear for any reasonable length of time.

Some automatic transmissions feature switchable 'economy,' 'sport,' and 'winter' modes. Economy usually implies a relaxed up- and down-change strategy, and is likely to be designed with best fuel economy in mind. With this setting, upward gear changes are made earlier, and the engine is also discouraged from revving close to its upper limit unless kickdown is demanded. If you're looking for best fuel economy and your gearbox has an 'economy' mode, use it!

A sport setting is usually designed to hold on to each gear longer as speed rises so the engine can achieve higher revs, and deliver more power. Sometimes it also alters kickdown settings, and with more modern units – in addition to perhaps altering accelerator pedal and even steering system responses – it can often force down-changes as speed declines on a trailing throttle, in anticipation of the driver demanding more power, more quickly. Whilst this type of setting may be useful for the driver in a hurry, it's hardly conducive to best possible fuel economy. Avoid sport settings when driving with economy in mind.

A winter setting is normally intended to help make a start in slippery conditions by selecting something other than first gear at rest, to make traction easier. Because its use is likely to be quite rare, the winter setting is unlikely to have any really noticeable effect on fuel economy when used as its designer intended.

Turn off unwanted things – and save ...

Modern cars feature lots of energy-hungry devices, energy that comes from the fuel in the tank. The more equipment you switch on, the more your fuel economy will suffer.

A particular offender here is the rear screen heater. Use it sparingly, and turn it off when the screen clears. Don't leave it on accidentally long after winter has gone, and – if your car has one – remember the same applies to electrically-heated front windscreens. Heated seats may be a winter luxury, but they too use lots of electricity, as do some powerful sound systems. The law defines situations when front and rear fog lights may be used – make sure they're turned off at other times. Switching electrical items off when they're not needed brings a worthwhile reward: better long-term fuel consumption ...

Air conditioning systems can place a significant load on the engine. Actual load depends on several variables, ranging from the weather in general to the difference between internal and external temperature, your chosen heating and ventilation settings, the type and rating of your particular car's system, and the level of sophistication of its control systems. Generally, engines consume rather more fuel when the air conditioning is switched on – especially if there's a noticeable difference between outside and inside temperatures. Such systems nonetheless have an important safety role in warm weather by keeping the driver comfortable, so best advice is never to forgo air conditioning completely in your search for maximum economy, but to attune yourself to the 'more air conditioning load means more fuel consumption' situation, balancing usage of such energy-consuming devices against actual need.

Always consider switching off the engine when stationary in abnormal traffic hold-ups. This is inevitably a matter for individual assessment depending on circumstances, using instinct and best judgement. Ordinary traffic lights, for instance, usually involve a relatively short wait, but some temporary lights produce lengthy delays, which might well justify switching off. If your traffic stream is held up by an accident or some visible incident, and you can see no-one's going anywhere any time soon, switch off immediately. If a delay is steadily lengthening towards 60 seconds with no sign of movement and no immediately obvious reason, it will probably be worth switching off.

Develop a sixth sense when travelling by keeping a watchful yet casual eye on traffic going in the opposite direction. Away from urban areas, heavy or light, free-flowing traffic has its own completely random character. Usually it's ever-present, but excites no real interest unless your kids are avid car or number-plate spotters. Yet for the astute driver, that comfortingly random stream can convey useful messages about conditions further down the road. If it changes to short streams of traffic followed by longer, completely empty stretches of road, you could be approaching temporary traffic lights, a slow moving tractor, an accident, or other obstruction. Slow down and be prepared. If gaps in a previously heavy traffic stream suddenly turn lengthy, with no vehicles passing in the other direction at all, it could mean serious trouble ahead, and the road may be blocked. Again, be prepared. A complete blockage is likely to mean a lengthy wait, and there might be a stationary queue of traffic, sitting just out of sight around the next bend.

Extra weight, extra drag, extra fuel – and extra pollution ...

Keep your car tidy and clutter-free, disposing of anything (except emergency items) unlikely to be needed on a regular basis. Periodically check the boot space, removing unnecessary tools and heavier items. If you run a four-wheel-drive vehicle, remove any bull-bars and side steps or side guards. Weight is certainly an enemy of best fuel economy, and some observers reckon that a workable rule of thumb is that each 100lb (220kg) carried in or on the car brings with it a 2 per cent fuel consumption penalty, and a corresponding increase in emissions.

Even the best roof boxes and racks introduce some wind resistance, adversely affecting fuel consumption. For best economy, always remove them when not in use.

This brings us to the fuel in the tank. If undertaking a long journey, fill up before departure, visiting the filing station when the engine is fully warm, and again only when the tank is at a low, but still safe, level. Don't risk running out of fuel on a motorway or other high speed road – fill up in good time, when, say, the gauge shows a quarter of a tank remaining. For day-to-day journeys, if weight can be minimised by keeping the fuel tank less than full for much of the time your vehicle is in use, it's worth doing so. However, this aspect can be something of a double edged sword. There's no point in returning to the filling station three times a week if a single fill-up would keep you going for the full seven days! If half a tank is sufficient for a typical week's motoring, don't put in more fuel than this each time. However, frequent visits to fill up may well involve going out of your way,

using fuel to get to the station, and once there, the job will inevitably involve more stopping, starting, engine idling and manoeuvring than if you hadn't visited the station in the first place ...

Anything outside the vehicle that's been added since it was styled by its maker is likely to have some negative effect on its aerodynamics – its wind resistance – which could bring a significant longer term fuel economy penalty. When travelling at higher speeds, it's worth remembering that an open sun roof, open windows and an empty roof rack all have adverse effects on economy, by breaking up the smooth airflow round the vehicle. Around town such things probably won't make a lot of difference, but the faster you go, the more impact they have. Shut sunroofs and windows whenever possible once above town speeds, since although air conditioning consumes some energy, it's generally a more fuel efficient option for keeping you cool when a car is moving quickly over longer distances.

Faster doesn't necessarily mean quicker – or sooner ...
It's a little known fact that on typical journeys of a few miles on today's crowded roads, driving as quickly as you can over the entire distance has little impact on your arrival time, compared to someone driving the same route more considerately and within the speed limits. For typical journeys such as a commute, while the safety risks are much higher, the difference in time taken will usually be measured in seconds. The difference in fuel consumption, however, will be quite noticeable. Restraint and patience are significant keys to better fuel economy. Whenever you're tempted to adopt a 'press-on regardless' driving style, ask yourself: do a few seconds matter that much?

Driving in today's world ...
Because many of the principles involved in saving fuel are closely related to those used in more advanced driving, adopting driving techniques aimed at improving fuel economy is also likely to have the effect of improving your safety as a driver. It's nonetheless very important that you don't compromise your safety, or that of other road users, whilst working on your economy driving skills.

One of the factors that an efficient driver will naturally wish to take into account is the weather, and if a particular journey is genuinely necessary. The performance, efficiency and fuel economy of internal combustion engines alters as the weather changes, but in normal circumstances the effects are very slight, and – since none of us can do much about it – can effectively be discounted. Windy conditions can have

a surprising impact on fuel economy: with a stiff westerly blowing, a journey along the M4 motorway from London to Bristol in a typical medium size car averaging 60mph might return 5-7mpg less than a journey in the opposite direction. Heading for Bristol, no matter how good the vehicle's aerodynamic design, the wind is a definite hindrance; heading east, it's a definite help. Either way, the impact on fuel economy is unavoidable.

Driving techniques aimed at optimising fuel economy can be practised with no great negative impact in a range of conditions, but you should always bear in mind that the weather can certainly make it either unreasonable or unsafe to continue using economy techniques to the irritation or detriment of other road users, or to road safety in general.

Though various situations might demand a move away from pure economy driving, winter conditions should give most food for thought. When the weather's bad, always be prepared to sacrifice fuel economy in the interests of road safety. An obvious example might be mistakenly avoiding use of the headlights (in a bid to save a tiny amount more fuel) when conditions are such that other motorists are using their lights, and the law (and indeed common sense) suggests that your lights should definitely be on.

Low temperatures, when frost, ice, and snow may be present or likely, also make it prudent to avoid rigorous application of economy driving techniques. Looking ahead well into the distance remains vitally important in such conditions, as roads that are in any way slippery invariably demand longer braking distances, bigger gaps between vehicles, lower speeds – not necessarily in higher gears – and plenty of caution. Driving in such conditions has been likened to driving on tiptoe, when it's really not about fuel economy, but about basic road safety! Be aware of changes in the weather, and don't hesitate to make more cautious progress if conditions turn tricky.

In days gone by, the technique of freewheeling (also called coasting) was often put forward as a means of saving fuel. Some cars came with built-in freewheel systems as standard, but for most drivers it simply involved selecting neutral (and sometimes turning off the engine altogether) to take advantage of downhill sections of road by allowing the vehicle to roll at its own – sometimes steadily quickening – pace. This technique was dangerous, and is even more dangerous now **as you could inadvertently lock the steering**!

Economically speaking, the practice probably springs from the long-gone days of petrol rationing. In carburetted petrol engines of that time, and indeed until as recently as the 1980s, fuel would continue to be drawn into the engine with the car in gear, on the overrun with the accelerator pedal released, typically while descending gradients. This situation (sometimes known as 'on a trailing throttle') resulted in very modest but (at the time) unavoidable fuel wastage. Selecting neutral – or better still, turning the engine off – reduced such wastage to very little or nothing at all. However, the restricted driver control resulting from a dead or idling engine whilst travelling at some speed was serious enough back then, before power assistance became as commonplace as it is today for major vehicle safety systems such as steering and braking. Indeed, some vehicles nowadays require engine power to operate their entire suspension systems.

Switching off the engine whilst on the move should be avoided at all costs, particularly with vehicles built

since the 1980s. You lose the ability to immediately accelerate if required in an emergency, and you will also lose all engine braking – a very useful weapon in an eco-driver's armoury. Worse, absence of engine power is very likely to precipitate a sudden change from normally light and easy to much heavier steering and braking systems, resulting when the usually ever-present power assistance is completely removed because of that 'dead' engine. Sometimes the effects can be delayed by several seconds – but whenever they happen, the sudden changes in the amount of effort needed to operate vital controls are likely to catch a driver totally unawares. If a powered suspension system is also involved, the comfortable ride and familiar precise handling qualities of the vehicle will also change dramatically. Any or all of these unexpected changes to the normally benign characteristics of the car could easily result in driver confusion – and a serious accident.

The advent of universal electronic fuel injection and engine management systems has completely put paid to any reason for attempting coasting or freewheeling in the name of fuel economy. **Whether driving a petrol, diesel or alternative-fuelled vehicle, in a nutshell, don't even think about turning off the engine whilst on the move or freewheeling downhill – there's absolutely no fuel-saving justification for attempting it.** Today's vehicle systems are sophisticated enough to detect any overrun situation when travelling downhill, and shut off the fuel supply to the engine for as long as it lasts, inconspicuously restoring fuel when either the driver demands power, or there is a requirement for the engine to idle as the vehicle comes to a stop. Don't switch off the engine whilst the vehicle is moving; it will not save any worthwhile amount of fuel, and it could endanger your safety and that of passengers and other road users.

Finally, always be prepared modify your driving style away from economy mode if such a move becomes appropriate – possibly vital – for the conditions. You might well have to temporarily sacrifice economy driving for road safety reasons at a moment's notice – **but do not hesitate to do so if it becomes necessary.** There'll be plenty more opportunities to practice your economy driving skills later.

How am I doing?
Since the early 1980s, fuel pumps in the UK have been required to display the quantity dispensed in litres, but in Britain, at least, the most easily understood measure of fuel consumption continues to be miles covered per gallon of fuel purchased. This means that checking your progress in becoming a more economical driver will involve a calculator and a little work – but the end will certainly justify the means. Use a diary to periodically record each fuel purchase in litres.

Progress towards improved fuel economy can be seen by refilling the tank to the same point each time, and noting the car's total mileage reading when doing so – or noting it over any preferred period of weeks or months. First, refill to a known, fixed, easily repeatable point in the fuel filler neck, if necessary creating your own visible mark, so that the same fill point can be achieved each time. If you want an average mpg figure over a greater distance than can be covered on one tank, then simply note in the diary the interim amounts (in litres) of fuel put in. Pump displays showing quantities dispensed are required to be accurate to close tolerances, so there's no real

need to fill to your chosen mark each time. Then, at the point when you want the overall mpg figure for the total distance covered, fill up to the chosen mark on the filler neck, and again note the mileage. Total up all quantities of fuel in litres added since that first fill up. Convert litres to gallons using a calculator (multiply litres by 0.2222), and work out the mileage travelled since the first fill up from the car's distance recorder. Divide the resulting mileage by the number of gallons (just converted from litres) to produce your mpg figure. By noting such results over a period of time, your mpg figures will show noticeable improvements as your economy driving style develops.

This calculation is good enough to get you started on the road to driving more economically, but the mpg figures it provides are unlikely to be deadly accurate. The gallons to litre conversion is one factor here, but a more significant error is introduced because car mileometers have unavoidable tolerances, which can incorporate errors approaching 10 per cent and still remain legal. As we shall see in a moment, other factors also introduce errors. The inevitable result when you perform your calculation is mpg figures that aren't quite as accurate as they should be. However, what we're looking for here primarily are genuine signs that the fuel bought is being stretched over greater distances, and calculating the results as described above will certainly show any such improvements over a period of time. A pin-point level of accuracy is unnecessary here because the car – including any in-built errors in distance recording – remains essentially the same, and the tank is being filled to the same point every time, so, assuming the vehicle is adequately maintained throughout, any changes observed must be the result of your new driving style.

If you really seek a more accurate indication of the car's miles per gallon figure, it's possible to go to far more extreme lengths. You can check the mileometer for errors, and if necessary apply a correction factor to the mileage readings shown each time you make an mpg calculation. To discover how accurate the distance recorder is, you'll need a convenient motorway, a calculator, a notebook, and a fairly patient passenger/observer. Make a trip of 16 kilometres (10 miles) on the motorway, with your observer counting the 100-metre marker posts at the edge of the hard shoulder to determine the exact distance. With 10 posts to a kilometre, this involves counting 160 posts. Either use a zeroed trip distance recorder, or have the observer make a careful note of the mileage readings on the speedometer at the precise moment the first and final 100 metre markers are passed. Best accuracy results from noting the distance to at least the nearest tenth of a mile. At the end of the run, subtract the first mileometer reading from the last, and convert the result to kilometres by multiplying it by 1.6. Note this resulting figure.

Next, enter the actual number of kilometres travelled (16) into the calculator, and divide it by the result achieved above. So, if at the completion of the run the mileometer was showing exactly 10 miles were travelled, you would enter 16, and divide it by 10x1.6 – that's 16 – as arrived at in the previous paragraph. The result here is 1, meaning the distance recorder is accurate and no correction factor is needed – a distance travelled multiplied by 1 comes to ... the distance travelled!

If, however, at the completion of your 16 kilometre run the mileometer was showing 10.5 miles travelled (an over-reading), you would divide the distance run by 10.5 multiplied by

1.6 – a result of 16.8. This means your mileage recorder shows that 16.8 kilometres were travelled – although the actual distance shown by the marker posts was only 16 kilometres. So, divide 16 by 16.8, and note down what will be your correction factor – 0.952380952.

To double check this is the right answer, apply this correction factor to the 10.5 miles travelled as shown on your mileometer. Enter 10.5 into the calculator, and multiply it by 0.952380952. The answer should be 10, the exact mileage equivalent of 16 kilometres – so everything checks out. In practice a correction factor of no more than three decimal places will usually be enough – 0.952 will provide quite sufficient accuracy.

So, in this example it would mean that each time you checked your mileage before a fuel consumption calculation, the distance shown as having been travelled since the last fill-up would need adjustment – by multiplying it by the correction factor. Whatever the mileage showing, multiplying by 0.952 will give the ACTUAL mileage travelled (rather than the mileometer reading), and it's this figure you should use in your mpg calculation for the most accurate result. Once the correction is made, the consumption in mpg can be calculated as shown earlier.

This example has shown a mileage recorder that was over-reading, so the correction factor is slightly less than 1. Mileage recorders may also under-read, in which case the correction factor will work out slightly over 1. However, the calculation required is exactly the same in either case.

There's always a catch ...
Nothing in motoring life is ever really simple. As we're talking best possible accuracy with these measurements

and calculations, some other variables might warrant consideration. Though it can take 20 or 30 thousand miles, tyres do wear, so their diameter alters slightly over their lifetime, and this will affect the mileometer reading. If you are really, really determined to take fuel economy measurement to the furthest degree, you could repeat the above calculations several times during the life of the tyres, apply a new correction factor at those intervals, and then average all the results.

Other factors that have a bearing are altitude and temperature, which can affect both fuel economy and engine performance. Even if you could find stretches of directly comparable road, in the mountains of Switzerland you would struggle hard to match the economy (or engine power output) delivered by the same car in the East Anglian fens. These effects are complex, and depend on various parameters. Most important are the laws of physics, but other influences include the fuel in use, whether a carburettor or fuel injection is used, whether the vehicle is normally aspirated or turbocharged, and whether it's fitted with an intercooler, as well as the overall level of sophistication of the engine management system.

There's an important variable that affects petrol cars in particular, but about which, in practice, even the best economy driver can do little: namely, the volume of fuel in the tank will vary according to temperature. In Britain, filling stations must by law store petrol underground, which keeps it quite cool, but being a highly volatile substance, it expands or contracts noticeably as temperatures rise or fall. For this reason alone, the distance travelled on successive tanks of fuel will always vary. However, the actual energy (which drives the car) contained in a particular volume of petrol does stay the same.

So, if the temperature underground is relatively high, the volume increases, and the fuel measured by the pump as it goes into your tank contains slightly less energy per gallon. If the underground temperature is lower next time around, you'll get more energy per gallon. In practice underground storage temperatures vary comparatively little, but the delivery of 'hot fuel' to filling stations can cloud this issue, and has long been a bone of contention in the retail petroleum industry, since it can adversely affect the number of litres delivered and paid for by the operator.

In straightforward terms, the cooler the petrol as it leaves the pump, the more energy will be contained in your refilled tank of fuel. If you follow Formula 1 racing, you may already know that this is the reason there are controls on the temperature of the fuel used by these cars. It is possible, in today's era of sophisticated electronics, to arrange for a petrol pump to automatically compensate for fuel temperature differences – thus ensuring the same amount of actual energy arrives in your tank for every fill up. The industry calls this 'standard temperature accounting,' and under this regime, a fuel quantity is pumped on the basis of its calculated volume at a temperature of 15 degrees Celsius. The resulting quantity is known as the 'standard litre,' and the methodology has been in use in Canada for some time. It is also due to become mandatory in some parts of Europe, though there is currently no legal requirement or even any plan to dispense fuel in this way at retail level in Britain. Nonetheless, the EU legislation covering the topic allows such pumps to be used here, so you may find new or refitted stations appearing with these latest pumps installed. If so, they should be clearly marked as dispensing the 'Standard Litre at 15 degrees C.'

Minimum Delivery 5 Litres
See That Indication Is Zero Before Delivery Commences

£ **24.44** This Sale

19.89 Litres

Volume corrected to 15°C
this does not apply for biodiesel

Only the inconspicuous wording "Volume corrected to 15°C" on the display reveals this as a standard temperature accounting (STA) fuel dispenser.

If you become aware of such a pump in your vicinity, always try and use it in your quest for optimum fuel economy – it will be a very helpful tool in ensuring consistent fuelling. Otherwise, use the same filling station pump as often as possible as your basis for fuel consumption calculations, to ensure the most reliable result in calculating vehicle economy.

Remembering that – recent tanker deliveries aside – underground temperatures probably won't change too much, filling up with petrol in the afternoon summer sunshine will result in the fuel expanding, which could lead to spillage during filling or soon afterwards. Apart from being potentially very dangerous, this will also waste some fuel if it overflows from the tank, upsetting your careful calculations. The safety issue here is quite straightforward: petrol is a highly flammable substance, and spillage, even of very small amounts, is something that should be avoided at all costs. Give some thought to when and where you fill up, and if you suspect

high ambient temperatures might cause problems, wait until the heat of the day is over before brimming the tank. Finally, do make sure the fuel tank filler cap is secure before restarting.

The importance of a properly maintained car

After driving style, probably the next most influential factor in the amount of fuel consumed by a car – and the amount and nature of its exhaust emissions – is the frequency and standard of its maintenance.

Diesel-engined vehicles may require rather more frequent servicing, and more frequent oil and filter changes, than their petrol equivalents. However, whether petrol or diesel, keeping up with routine vehicle servicing is vital in the long term quest for fuel efficiency. Such things as a blocked air filter can have a major effect on fuel economy and exhaust emission. They are inexpensive to replace, and should receive attention at manufacturer-specified intervals. A handbrake that fails to release completely has the effect of braking the rear wheels slightly at all times, increasing the vehicle's rolling resistance, and requiring extra fuel to overcome this.

Modern electronic systems keep an engine working efficiently far longer than was the case a few years ago, but that doesn't mean engine maintenance can safely be forgotten. It's vital that routine service periods are adhered to if a vehicle is to deliver optimum economy and lowest emissions in the long term. At least once a year, ask your garage to carry out an electronic engine health-check to find out how the engine is performing against its maker's intentions. Try very hard to ensure your vehicle is always in the best of mechanical health.

The driver has control of some vehicle servicing aspects affecting fuel consumption – indeed, in some cases the law insists that such things are the driver's direct responsibility. Ensure you have a copy of the car's handbook, and be aware of those responsibilities. Make a particular note of the type of engine oil required, and use only the recommended grade when topping up. Bear in mind, however, that with some vehicles it may be possible to gain some economy advantages by switching to a 'synthetic' engine oil. This has the potential to improve fuel consumption, but because of a risk of engine damage, it is certainly not a switch to make without appropriate professional advice. Start by reading the vehicle handbook, and follow up with a visit to the service department of an accredited dealer for your car. It may also be possible to gain information from the customer service operation of the manufacturer or importer.

Be aware of the part that tyres play, and the importance of the correct tyre size, specification, types, and working pressures for your car. Note down the pressures required, and keep the note easily accessible in the car. Some makers affix a tyre pressure information label inside the driver's door frame. If it's not there, attach your own as an easy reminder. Bear in mind that tyre pressures may require altering for heavier loads or sustained long-distance work, and adjust them accordingly. Tyres affect not only the safety and driveability of the vehicle, but also its fuel consumption, too. The wrong type or size of tyres, or tyres at the wrong pressures, not only have huge safety implications but could also result in higher fuel consumption. Check and adjust them no less than once a week, when the car has been standing for at least 12 hours, and never leave tyre pressures unchecked for weeks at a time. Some modern cars are fitted with automatic tyre-pressure monitoring, but while useful, this should not be regarded as a reason to avoid manually checking tyre pressures at regular intervals.

Tyres come in sizes and speed ratings for very specific jobs. Make sure your car has the correct specification of tyres to match its use and performance. A modest hatchback and a turbocharged seven-seater MPV could have the same wheel sizes, but the tyres fitted will be very different. Some modern tyres are specially designed to reduce fuel consumption through low rolling resistance. For ultimate fuel economy, find out if any are available for your car, and fit them next time new tyres are required.

If you do not have a suitable driver's handbook for your car, try to obtain one from the parts department of the main dealer for the particular vehicle type. Handbooks tend to remain available for only a limited time after a particular vehicle model ceases production, and supplies sometimes dry up even while vehicles are still available. An internet search may find owners' clubs or independent outlets able to supply such manuals. There are also various specialists offering handbooks for vehicles of the past – sometimes a long way into the past. These include www.manualsource.co.uk, www.pooksmotorbooks.co.uk, and www.instruction-manuals.co.uk.

Gadgets

Since the advent of the motor car, an unceasing desire to improve fuel economy has been one of the most fertile of breeding grounds for imaginative ideas. The result has been a long succession of aftermarket gadgets, claiming to deliver improved fuel economy with minimal driver effort. Invariably these devices have involved a cash outlay, sometimes of a significant amount. The principles on which most have been claimed to operate have usually been opaque, clouded in secrecy by inventors and manufacturers – but most have followed a 'fitted in minutes with no technical knowledge – and get an extra x mpg' philosophy. Marketing material was thus curiously coy about descriptive detail, though techniques have ranged from magic potions poured into fuel tanks to water injection, and the alleged effect of strategically-placed magnets on the alignment of molecules in the fuel flowing from the tank into the engine.

At the peak of their popularity in the 1960s, '70s, and early '80s, some startling claims about improvements were being made for add-on economy devices. Plenty of independent testing was carried out by well-qualified organisations in tightly controlled circumstances, but with little by way of repeatable improvements apparently being demonstrated in the laboratory or realised on the road. Though they still spring up from time to time, the arrival of complex, electronically-controlled fuel injection systems and tightened emissions regulations has largely sounded the death knell for such devices and equipment, since their fitment and fuel system integration have become much less straightforward without specialist knowledge.

Whilst the phrase 'never say never' comes to mind as far as add-on economy gadgets are concerned, 50 years of history and experience have demonstrated pretty effectively that far more fuel can be saved through application of efficient driving techniques than through investing hard-earned cash in one of motoring's better-known lost causes. The level of knowledge, skill, and expertise applied to the design of modern fuel injection systems and vehicle engines by motor manufacturers means that every avenue to optimise economy within today's stringent regulations is thoroughly researched, long before a vehicle reaches retail customers. In today's hugely competitive market, little scope remains for any 'magic formula.' It's a pretty safe bet that if manufacturers could find an easy way to stay within the legislative rules and offer still better fuel economy in subsequent generations of vehicles, they would do just that!

Are all fuels the same?

In a word, no ... although there are many shades of grey. This is a very complex subject, much of which is outside the scope of this book. Clearly, petrol and diesel fuels are absolutely not the same, and nor are LPG, compressed natural gas, and so on. Yet it might be tempting for the non-technical driver to regard all products described as 'petrol' as much the same – and all diesel as similar, too – based on the notion that all petrol vehicles will surely run on fuel described as petrol, and all diesel vehicles on something described as diesel. A note of caution here: these are very sweeping generalisations indeed, and they are not entirely or automatically true in either case, even varying depending on where in the world you happen to be filling up.

There was a time, particularly in the 1960s and '70s, when car fuels – then almost exclusively petrol – were the subject of heavy marketing by the major oil companies. The rapid growth of TV advertising brought Esso's famous slogan "I've got a tiger in my tank" to the masses, while "VIP, the spirit of modern motoring" was heavily promoted as the fuel of choice for "the man with more miles to make." (There weren't so many female licence holders back then ...) These campaigns, backed by catchy jingles and everything from tie-on tiger's tails to 'Make Money banknotes' and offers of multiple Green Shield stamps, were born of strenuous efforts to develop and maintain brand loyalty amongst motorists. However, over time the motoring public grew weary. As long as it was from a pump marked with the right number of 'stars,' fuel came to be regarded as, well, fuel. Whether it was 'Shell with ICA' or 'Cleveland Discol with alcohol,' or any other of the multitudinous brands then available, apart from occasional (usually negative) exceptions, the family car went much the same, no matter from whose pump the fuel had come. Gradually, as prices rose, brand loyalty faded, and price savings of a few pence became far more significant. This was quite unlike, say, baked beans, where you might taste a difference between brands, and thus be prepared to pay more for one than another. This situation still prevails today, and with the advent of clear, unambiguous marking of fuel dispensers and well-defined regulations closely controlling fuel quality and

quantity at all stages from refinery to forecourt, customers have never been more assured about the product being purchased.

So, generic types of fuels today are essentially similar – but only up to a defined point. The overall performance of petrol, rated by its Research Octane Number (RON) used throughout Europe, can certainly be expected to be broadly similar in propelling a vehicle, as a result of meeting those well-defined standards. If your car is rated to use 95 RON unleaded fuel, barring unfortunate accidents (which do happen, regrettably), no matter who supplied it or the actual brand on the forecourt, what comes out of a pump thus marked will generally suit your car. Quite rightly, this allows non-technical purchasers full confidence in vehicle refuelling.

Yet, just like the days of the 2 to 5 star ratings now consigned to history, alternative fuel grades are in use. In some parts of Europe, 91 Octane unleaded petrol is widely available, and many new cars supplied into those markets are set up to use it without difficulty. Such fuel may, however, lead to anything from slight loss of performance to potential damage if used continuously in an engine designed to run on 95 Octane unleaded or higher, as is usual in Britain. For optimum performance, economy, and emissions – and minimised risk of engine damage – it thus remains important that the correct petrol grade is used to fill the tank.

A non-technical driver really doesn't need to know the precise difference between the widely-used, 95 RON-rated unleaded, and its lower performance 91 RON or higher performance 98 RON relations. It is enough to just know that there is a genuine difference. Vehicle handbooks will always indicate appropriate fuels, but today only a few higher performance vehicles gain any useful benefits from 98 RON unleaded fuel, and there's no economy or performance benefit in using it – invariably at a premium price – in a vehicle designed to use the lower-rated 95 RON fuel.

Leaded fuel

Whatever its actual RON rating, the unleaded petrol available across Europe represents a return to the earliest years of motoring, when the only vehicle fuel available was ... unleaded petrol. As the search for increased engine power progressed, a small amount of lead was added, mainly (though not exclusively) as an aid to preventing what was called 'knock' or 'pinking,' which can be detrimental to an engine. Leaded fuel prevailed for many years after the Second World War, until the advent of exhaust catalysts – and growing environmental and health concerns over airborne lead. Catalysts play a major part in reducing pollution levels from vehicle engines, and are damaged by the presence of even small amounts of lead in the engine's exhaust stream.

Matters came to a head during the 1980s, when a decision was taken to introduce unleaded fuel to forecourts, ahead of the mandatory installation of exhaust catalysts on new petrol cars which took effect in 1991. To allow reasonable service life from vehicles capable of running only on leaded fuel, in Britain both types continued on sale until January 2000, at which point lead as a fuel additive was outlawed by legislation. 'Lead replacement petrol' (LRP) was then offered instead, containing additives allowing most engines that could not be converted to unleaded fuel to continue operating. By 2003, sales of LRP were dwindling rapidly, becoming an uneconomic retail proposition by the end of the

In the 1950s and 1960s, additives were used as enticements to particular fuel brands. Shell's magic ingredient was 'ICA,' as displayed on this defunct pump.

year. Midway through 2004, LRP had vanished from British forecourts forever.

Leaded four star fuel remains available in very small quantities in Britain through a formal dispensation awarded to one distributor. It's supplied through a limited network of independent filling stations, for owners of classic vehicles wishing to preserve the originality of what today can be extremely valuable machinery. As an alternative, it remains possible to purchase an additive to mix with each tank of fuel, allowing most engines originally designed to run on leaded petrol to continue in use where, for some reason, they cannot be successfully converted to run on unleaded.

Diesel
Diesel carries a rarely seen 'cetane' rating, which in outline might be regarded as similar to petrol's octane rating. Again, vehicle owners have no great need for a technical understanding of such ratings, which are largely irrelevant for UK car drivers, since only one grade (rated a minimum cetane of 51) is routinely available on forecourts. For the private vehicle user, the only other significant variables that might be of interest are so-called 'red diesel' and 'winter diesel.' An additive (not a fuel) often known by its registered trade name 'Adblue,' first introduced for diesel-engined commercial vehicles, is now also finding its way into the diesel-powered private car arena.

Winter conditions can lead to a particular problem with diesel. At low ambient temperatures, it has a tendency to turn into something more like a wax than an oil. If left unchecked, this results in poor running or very difficult starting – often both – since the fuel simply will not flow as a liquid when temperatures fall too low. Vehicle manufacturers address this at the design stage by ensuring that fuel lines are not routed in external areas where frost may affect them, occasionally even resorting to electrical heating of some fuel system components if such problems are anticipated. For their part, fuel refiners make supplies of winter diesel available in the distribution network from around October to May. This contains a specific additive to mitigate against the waxing effect in winter temperatures; in Britain,

diesel is thus rendered useable down to temperatures around -15 to -18 degrees Celsius.

Red diesel contains a marker dye, and is supplied only to authorised users. It's extensively used by powered farm implements, tractors, and marine engines, and, as a concession to the industries concerned, is supplied on a taxation-rebated arrangement to users of such equipment. The very significant taxation reduction involved means its use is not allowed in vehicles intended for normal road use, where fuels are always subject to full current taxation policy. Her Majesty's Customs and Revenue department carries out frequent spot checks on vehicles in appropriate areas to ensure red diesel is not in use in road vehicles. There have been several high-profile cases involving inappropriate red diesel usage, and the penalties for misuse are severe. If the concentration is high enough, red diesel fuel appears a pinkish colour, though when mixed with ordinary diesel, chemical analysis is often necessary to determine whether red diesel is contained in the mixture.

Thus, there are various distinct lines of demarcation between fuels found on today's forecourts. Yet there are other differences within these – petrol or diesel, each oil company's offering is essentially unique. For a start, the crude oil from which the product has been refined may well have come from different oil fields around the world, so the basic chemical composition could be different. Also, each oil company blends various additives into its product – the result of its long-term brand development. These might range from dyes giving the fuel a particular colour through to complex chemicals designed to aid combustion or prolong engine life, and, in diesel, an anti-frothing agent. The driver paying for the fuel will rarely consider such things; differentiating between brands is impossible when you don't see or taste it, and you don't strip the engine down to see the effect on its internals as mileage increases. It's quite impossible for ordinary motorists to scientifically compare precise mpg or wear and tear resulting from one brand versus another in the controlled conditions of a laboratory. Today, fuel going in the tank hardly merits any thought beyond cost – it could be the colour of a rainbow, and you'd never know. It could be good, bad, or indifferent for the long-term health of the engine, and still you'd never know. This is where the 'all fuels must be the same' philosophy originates, and why today, for so many motorists, price is the only fuel characteristic that really matters ...

Nonetheless, aided by glossy marketing, some suppliers have moved the fuel quality differential a stage further, launching new brands such as Esso Supreme, Shell V-power, Total Excellium and BP Ultimate. These have been marketed as more 'advanced' fuels than Britain's standard 95 RON forecourt offering, with a range of claimed benefits not included with 'ordinary' fuels. Taking as an example BP Ultimate petrol, introduced in Britain in 2003: this product is rated at 102 RON, and is claimed by its maker to deliver up to 50 per cent more internal engine cleaning power, making it more efficient in operation over a longer period of time. Tests are said to have shown the resultant reduction in engine 'clogging' improves performance, and also brings a fuel economy improvement of up to 25 miles from a full tank. Other claims have included sharper acceleration, improved responsiveness, and less harmful emissions, particularly carbon monoxide and hydrocarbons. Most of the tests aimed at demonstrating the benefits of BP Ultimate were carried out by respected independent laboratories, including Britain's Millbrook facility and Ricardo engineering, as well as at BP's own facilities.

At its launch, this fuel received endorsement from the Department of Transport and Ford in Britain, but comprehensive tests by the well-regarded *What Car?* magazine in 2007 did not show it – or its immediate contemporaries – living up to improved economy claims. In real-world tests for the magazine by a former senior research engineer for the AA, Peter de Nayer, high-octane premium fuels including BP Ultimate, Shell V-Power, Esso Supreme and Total Excellium were reported to perform little or no better than their cheaper equivalents, despite costing around 7 per cent more per litre.

The magazine's editor felt the tests showed premium fuels were "an unnecessary expense with no major fuel economy benefit." Sainsbury's 97-octane product was the top-performing fuel in *What Car?*'s tests, and was found to deliver 0.5mpg more than its 95-octane fuel – in real terms, the magazine claimed, that meant just 6 miles more per tank. Its overall verdict was: "Drivers who fill their cars with expensive 'superfuels' and expect to see big economy gains should think again ... Even using the fuel companies' own figures, you're unlikely to travel 7 per cent further on a tank of fuel for a 7 per cent increase in your fuel bill." Yet in the years since these various fuels have been launched, the internet has been alive with complimentary comments from apparently satisfied users ...

The jury thus remains undecided on whether such 'superfuels' really deliver on the promises made. Over a complete period of car ownership, it may be that benefits in mechanical efficiency, engine longevity, and fuel economy will become more apparent. Individual drivers, steadfastly choosing and using such fuels in the long term, are best placed to assess whether the claimed benefits are delivered – while outweighing the financial disadvantages involved. Real though they may be in terms of superior formulation, the big question is whether 'superfuels' are, at heart, simply a return to an era of marketing hype so beloved of the fuel industry in years gone by. Only you can be the judge of that.

Making use of information
Through the internet, information on virtually any topic under the sun is nowadays almost instantly available, and that includes vehicle fuel economy and economical driving generally. A few of the principal sources are noted here, although new sources are appearing all the time, waiting to be uncovered. An internet search will soon reveal plenty of sites that could help anyone looking to become a more economical, less polluting driver.

Impartial advice on car fuel economy is available in all new car showrooms, produced by the Department for Transport under EU directives. New vehicles come with a coloured chart showing the emissions band into which that vehicle falls, the cost of a vehicle excise licence for it, and other useful information. Another helpful source of information for new car buyers is a booklet published by the Vehicle Certification Agency (VCA). This lists the emission and fuel consumption figures of all new cars on the British market, and contains a range of useful facts on cars and the atmospheric pollution they generate, along with details of the increasingly stringent test regimes now being applied. It's available on the internet at www.vca.gov.uk, and you can use the VCA's Car Fuel Database (www.vcacarfueldata.org.uk)

to seek out your ideal fuel efficient car. Searches can be undertaken based on fuel economy, tax band, and car make or model.

The Society of Motor Manufacturers and Traders (SMMT) offers useful information concerning fuel economy and emissions on its website, www.smmt.co.uk. A helpful booklet called *Drive Green, Drive Safely* is available to download.

Various other public and private organisations provide helpful information and advice on economy and emissions. They include the Department for Transport (www.dft.gov.uk), which has a special section on its website called 'Act on CO_2.' This is available at www.dft.gov.uk/actonCO2

An eco-safe driving style is also being promoted by the Driving Standards Agency (www.dsa.gov.uk). Other helpful websites are offered by the AA (www.theaa.com), the RAC Foundation (www.racfoundation.org), the Institute of Advanced Motorists (www iam.org.uk) the Energy saving trust (www.est.org.uk). The Green Car website(www.thegreencarwebsite.co.uk) and www.cleangreencars.co.uk are concerned with emissions and pollution issues, while registering with www. petrolpricescom will bring regular updates on the cheapest fuel prices around the country. This site also provides some fuel saving tips.

A gradually unfolding world of greener, more economical driving is bringing with it increasing amounts of helpful information. Most of it is free, and yours for the taking. Seek it out and make use of it ...

New opportunities to save fuel and reduce pollution: how technology can help economical driving
Without the help of modern, inbuilt electronic systems today's cars

would be far less reliable, much less economical, and certainly more polluting than they are. But aside from features already 'designed in,' there are various other helpful and readily available aids which can further help fuel economy: some are optional features available on new cars, others are available in the aftermarket for fitment by dealers or accessory companies. If you're buying a used car, make sure you have a copy of the original drivers manual, so that you can be aware of the correct operation of all the standard and optional equipment which is fitted to it. Such equipment might include ...

Trip computers
These can be very helpful devices for the driver seeking best fuel economy, and they feature on increasing numbers of new cars as standard. If a trip computer is not standard equipment, it can often be specified on a new vehicle as an option at relatively modest cost.

Modern trip computers offer a comprehensive range of functions, usually including helpful indications of instantaneous and average fuel consumption, and predicted distance to an empty tank. In driving for maximum fuel economy, whilst 'instantaneous mpg' can be of use in helping a driver to immediately and constantly appreciate how different driving styles and road conditions impact upon fuel use, the 'average mpg' readout is likely to be of most interest. This is because the ability to easily reset the computer to zero at any time allows a driver to determine the fuel economy achieved on any complete individual trip or longer period of use, taking into account the full range of driving conditions. Some systems separately allow cumulative average fuel economy to be displayed, which might be used to indicate fuel consumption over a week or a month's motoring, or over the life of each tank of fuel. All can be useful in analysing whether your attempts to drive more economically are proving successful – and gradually improving mpg figures

Trip computers help to make efficient progress. Information here includes average fuel consumption, distance to empty, radio channel, external temperature, and trip and total mileages. (Courtesy Reg Burnard)

also provide tangible encouragement to do better still ...

Despite their reliance on modern technology, trip computers, whilst being a very useful tool for the economy-minded driver, are by no means perfect, and are unlikely to be calibrated for particularly high accuracy in the average mass-produced car. The most likely cause of errors in such mpg readouts is the system's reliance on measures of distance and fuel flow, which themselves may not be accurate for a variety of reasons. However, the fact that any built-in errors are likely to remain relatively constant over a period of time does allow the readings gained – and any improvements seen – to be usefully comparable with each other. Nonetheless, unless proven otherwise by real-world testing, it's as well to treat any 'Distance to empty' (DTE) readouts with a degree of scepticism, as fuel remaining dwindles below a quarter of a tank. Just like the traditional analogue-style fuel gauge, trip computers rarely provide good 'distance to empty' accuracy at the lower end of the scale.

Here, with the fuel gauge edging closer to the red zone at empty, you may notice the remaining distance shown on the trip computer display declines much more quickly than the vehicle's typical fuel consumption rate. This is a safeguard to encourage you to fill up without delay, though even when the display begins its final warning sequence there could still be anything up to 50 or 60 miles range remaining. Just don't push your luck too far!

Satellite navigation
The cheapest way to navigate seems likely to remain a road atlas, but if you frequently travel in unfamiliar areas or can't work a map very well, satellite navigation could help you avoid taking a wrong turning – which, of course, has an immediate fuel consumption penalty. Such systems can be a very helpful aid to both road safety and improved fuel economy, but it's always worth bearing

This fitted sat nav system offers 'birds-eye' mapping, with Traffic Message Channel integration. Height above sea level, time and temperature information is also displayed.

in mind that, even when regularly updated, they are certainly not infallible.

Portable systems now start well under £200, though some sophisticated manufacturer-fitted systems can cost thousands. Many top-end cars now include satellite navigation as standard, and some incorporate a helpful addition called Traffic Message Channel (TMC). This allows the navigation system to recalculate a chosen route, when it (silently) receives news of problems or hold-ups on a route it is already traversing. This function can reduce delay enormously, with the driver simply following alternative roads, avoiding what otherwise might be a time (and fuel) consuming delay on the original route.

If you are buying a vehicle with satellite navigation fitted, do read and understand the manual to ensure you get the best from it. Some inbuilt systems are quite complex, and the existence of the TMC facility, and various other helpful features such as storage of recent relevant traffic messages, or hotel and fuel station location data – even the ability to automatically summon help in an emergency situation – may not be immediately apparent, and might otherwise be missed.

Operator-assisted navigation and assistance systems

Several variations on the basic satellite navigation theme have been developed. Many of these alternatives are based around direct contact with an operator centre, from which a route to a chosen destination may be downloaded into the car and followed in the normal way. Some systems allow enquiries about such things as restaurant bookings and the location of hotels and petrol stations; others can automatically summon emergency assistance when an accident involves the triggering of vehicle safety systems such as airbags.

Cruise control

Cruise control is increasingly appearing as a standard fitment on new cars, and is often a modestly-priced option where not already included. With thoughtful use it certainly helps deliver improved fuel economy on longer journeys, particularly when light traffic allows easy cruising. It does, however, come with a slight fuel consumption penalty if used indiscriminately. Cruising a level road, such equipment will be far better than a typical driver at maintaining a steady throttle setting and hence the desired cruising speed (and best fuel economy). This is because human beings are incapable of holding a foot absolutely steady on an accelerator pedal for minutes on end. Any change in pedal setting leads to some – normally slight – speed variations, which in turn leads to slight additional fuel consumption as speed varies.

Travelling downhill, there will be relatively little effect on actual fuel consumption whether a human being or cruise control is operating the accelerator. However, going uphill, the human driver can steal an advantage over cruise control in minimising consumption. This is because cruise control is designed to unwaveringly maintain speed, up hill and down dale. Clearly more fuel is used climbing hills at a maintained speed (effectively depressing the accelerator to offset speed otherwise lost by climbing the incline) than it would if the throttle setting was held absolutely steady, and speed gradually declined.

For absolute maximum economy on faster roads, and as long as it doesn't inconvenience other traffic, it may be worth disengaging cruise control on the more severe upward inclines, and trading off some cruising speed for a slightly slower ascent. The difference between a 60mph and 70mph ascent in time terms will be insignificant in a long journey, but fuel savings will accumulate each time.

Cruise control is something of an acquired taste at first, but a little time spent acclimatising will pay useful dividends, and in time its use will probably become almost second nature. The benefits in both improved fuel economy and reduced numbers of speeding transgressions are significant: cruise control brings a fuss-free air to motorway and main road travel, and is a particular boon in lengthy 40 or 50mph speed limits, where it prevents speed creeping slowly upward to illegal levels.

Adaptive cruise control is a recent development of 'ordinary' cruise control, which uses active, radar-based technology to monitor vehicle speed and make adjustments to maintain a predetermined (and often driver selectable) safe distance between you and the vehicle ahead. The operating principle does, however, involve variations in cruising speed to maintain the selected gap, a characteristic that may have some slightly negative effect on overall fuel economy.

Active systems like this can provide immediate warnings about rapidly changing conditions – for example, if the vehicle in front suddenly performs an emergency stop. Some systems are even capable of applying braking if necessary, but a driver must always be alert to the fact that no electronic system has yet managed to defy the laws of physics, and things happen very quickly at 70mph – that's over 100 feet (30.4 metres) per second.

The moral is: like all vehicle

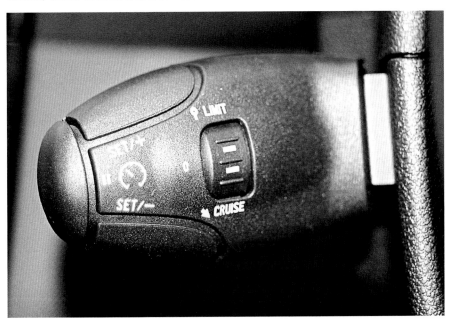

Cruise control on cars is increasingly common; speed limiters are much rarer. This Peugeot system offers both, all controlled from a single stalk.

systems, cruise control can be useful in assisting the driver, but the driver is always in control of the car. A founding principle of economical driving – looking further ahead while developing a keener sense of anticipation to deliver optimum car control – is at its peak in motorway and dual carriageway travel. In seeking better fuel economy, cruise control can certainly be considered an aid, but a driver must always remain alert to changing conditions on the road ahead – and avoid at all costs becoming a slave to cruise control's deceptive charms ...

Speed limiters

Some vehicles offer a switchable cruise control or speed limiter system, which can be set by the driver in either mode as required, displaying relevant selections in the instrument display. Speed limiters have a useful safety role all the way from the urban environment to the national motorway network, but they also deliver a fuel economy bonus. If you spend considerable time in a 30 or 40mph speed limit, why risk burning more fuel by constantly exceeding this? Set the limiter whenever you can, to restrict both the fuel used and the chances of a penalty ticket.

Stop and start

Automatic engine stop and start systems have been available on some passenger cars for a number of years, and have their original roots as far back as the 1980s. Though a variety of systems are available today, all work in a similar way, to automatically stop an idling engine as a vehicle comes to a halt, typically in town traffic, and restart it very rapidly as soon as the driver releases the footbrake and presses the accelerator pedal. An inhibitor switch allows the driver to de-select the system as required. To achieve high levels of

reliability, vehicles so fitted invariably incorporate modifications to cope with the increased stresses imposed on starter and electrical system components.

In practice, while a driver may initially find it slightly unnerving having the engine stop each time the vehicle comes to rest in heavy traffic, the restart times typically achieved are so rapid that, to all intents and purposes, the vehicle can be driven perfectly normally throughout.

Improvements in both fuel consumption and emissions are claimed to be typically in the order of some 5 to 8 per cent over an identical car lacking such equipment, but naturally a lot depends on the vehicle usage. Clearly a car used predominantly in an urban area during rush hours is likely to show greater savings here than one used almost exclusively on long distance, high-speed journeys involving light traffic and few stops. Often however, such stop/start systems are installed in combination with other devices, allowing the vehicle to show further emission and consumption benefits away from urban areas.

Trafficmaster

This company operates a nationwide network of traffic sensors in Britain, with incoming information constantly collated and updated to provide a 'real time' picture of congestion on the main road and motorway network. Subscribers to the service receive constant updates on actual average traffic speeds in areas of particular interest. Such information could prove invaluable in planning routes to maximise fuel economy, while minimising pollution and avoiding congestion.

A word about older vehicles ...

Most technological innovations

mentioned here apply to cars manufactured in the relatively recent past. The older the car, the poorer its overall environmental performance is likely to be, and size for size, it probably won't be as economical in its use of fuel. Their technology may be less advanced, but older vehicles can of course still be driven in an economical way, and the maxim remains: the less fuel you use, the less pollution you will cause.

New developments – and the future
As technology moves forward, manufacturers are able to provide inbuilt equipment capable of giving a driver increasing amounts of helpful information about the vehicle's fuel efficiency. Such developments are ultimately limited only by the ability to gather, process and display suitable data, the imagination of the system designers, and the availability of appropriate technology to enact their new designs.

A few systems already available are capable of offering a driver useful economy data both dynamically whilst the vehicle is in use, and as a 'review' at the completion of a journey. Honda, for instance, includes an 'Ecological drive assist' system in its Insight hybrid model. An 'EcoN' button on the dashboard activates a specific, optimised mode

Honda's Insight provides information on the vehicle's current, recent and long-term fuel efficiency. It also rates driver eco-performance for each journey!

Fiat's 'eco:Drive' system is a sophisticated, downloadable, eco-efficiency monitor. This display relates to an Italian-market, CNG-powered vehicle, but conventional fuels are similarly covered.

supporting more fuel-efficient driving by controlling the engine, CVT, and other powertrain components to best economy advantage. It also adjusts the air conditioning unit, extends idle 'stop' time, and increases regenerative recharging during deceleration, further enhancing fuel efficiency. Alongside this, the new car's inbuilt electronic systems are sophisticated enough to 'score' a drivers economy performance for every trip. Data can also be provided on fuel efficiency over the full life of the car.

Meanwhile, Fiat is steadily developing its in-car 'eco:Drive' system, intended to help drivers easily understand the impact of their driving on both fuel consumption and CO_2 emissions. Using a USB stick plugged into the car's dashboard, the system records detailed data about the vehicle and how it is being driven, which can later be uploaded on to a computer. In turn, this can provide an analysis of the driver's performance on that or other recent journeys, along with suggestions on methods to improve efficiency.

Drivers using the Fiat system have access to an online community to discuss ideas, offer feedback, and suggest improvements – with the manufacturer already responding with updates and enhancements to the system. Initially available on a very limited number of models, the scope of the technology is being widened to include commercial vehicles, where potential for improving fuel economy and reducing emissions is considerable.

Elsewhere, future developments in satellite navigation technology could pay further dividends for the eco-

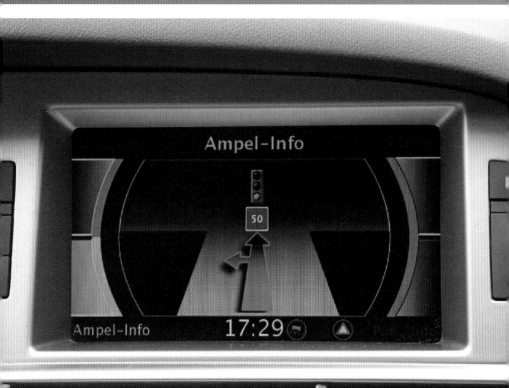

Audi's prototype Travolution system could help reduce congestion and pollution by indicating how to pass through a whole series of traffic lights on green. (Courtesy Audi UK)

conscious driver. Technology known as 'eco-routing' is becoming available, allowing provision of a route computed with a priority regard to how much fuel might be used in traversing it. Some satellite navigation systems now offer the ability to plan such journeys, while the website www.viamichelin.co.uk – part of the Michelin tyre empire – may be of help in planning particularly economical routes.

Additional processing power linked to and integrated with further-developed satellite navigation and TMC facilities will ultimately allow in-car systems to take account of driving style, select the best roads to use, anticipate likely delays and idling time, and even consider the health of the engine during the journey, so that optimum fuel economy can be achieved for the route being driven.

Further ahead, combining these types of functions could further maximise conservation of fuel and the lowering of emissions on all car journeys. Uploading real-time 'big picture' data on completed or unfinished journeys to other vehicles following the same route could bring economy and pollution benefits, and also enhance the quality of data being processed, further refining the techniques of 'eco-routing,' which as yet are at a relatively early stage in terms of dynamic possibilities. This has led to industry discussions about hitherto isolated vehicles being considered as part of a network, in a direct parallel with wi-fi computer technology. If, in future, vehicles were interconnected directly by short range radio to other vehicles nearby and the outside world in general, via, say, a 'mo-fi' system, it could allow the sending, receiving, and processing of recent journey and traffic data, from which improved fuel economy, reduced pollution, and the avoidance of traffic hold-ups could be just some of many possible benefits.

German manufacturer Audi is supporting experimental work in this direction, with its long-term 'Travolution' project involving traffic management experts in the brand's German home town of Ingolstadt. The intention is to dramatically reduce the number of stops needed at red lights by creating a communications link between cars and the traffic light network, thus improving synchronisation and phasing of traffic light networks as a whole. In turn, this will streamline urban traffic flow and reduce CO_2 emissions.

Data transmitters built into each traffic light send messages to cars in the vicinity, alerting them to the time remaining until the next green phase. The car's onboard system then calculates the speed that must be maintained to pass through the light during its green phase, and displays this inside the car.

A network of 46 'intelligent' traffic lights has been installed in the centre of Ingolstadt, some of which have already been upgraded to enable communication with specially modified vehicles provided as part of a €1.2 million pilot project. More cars and many more traffic light installations are to be incorporated as the project evolves.

Searching your soul
On the roads today you'll find drivers with a wide range of skills and attitudes, from the haphazard to the thoughtful, and on to the highly advanced. There are speeding drivers, sly drivers, slow drivers, timid drivers, aggressive drivers, bullish drivers, threatening drivers, incompetent drivers, hesitant drivers, courteous drivers, impatient drivers, and plenty more besides. We've all heard tales of genuine road rage, and many will have experienced it first hand: we've all felt like tearing hair out at the antics of others on the roads. Most drivers will not claim to be experts or advanced – they are more likely to think of themselves as 'good' – but in truth, most just want to get to their destination as soon as they can, and they'd be very much happier if you didn't get in the way ...

But this brings an uncomfortable thought: next time you take to the roads, YOU will be one of those drivers. How do you shape up?

As you set out to burn less fuel as a result of a more carefully considered driving style, you might well believe almost every other road user is out there with the sole aim of preventing you from doing this. Until now, you perhaps coped with traffic or driver problems through a combination of irritation, agitation or excitement, maybe even a gesture or an expletive or two, later recounting tales to your friends or family of the strange, unacceptable, or downright stupid behaviour you experienced today on the road.

Here we come to the final part of the challenge to become a more economical, more efficient, and indeed more caring driver. It won't be easy, for it involves you being honest and determined enough to look very closely at how you drive right now, and what you can do to change things for the better. So, it's time to confront entrenched attitudes head on, to revisit and analyse your motoring prejudices, your skill level and your current driving habits. Get extra professional training to restore skills or confidence if you need to, and then start to adapt, modify and develop your own particular, considered, and more ecologically friendly view of the motoring universe.

Better day-to-day fuel economy involves the consistent application of a rather different approach to general driving, and unless you already have some previous experience in the field, it will almost certainly take some conscious effort to modify what has become your natural driving style. Some aspects – like choosing the right car, adequate vehicle maintenance, absorbing helpful information and harnessing new technology – are entirely practical cornerstones, foundations on which you can build. But as we've seen, the driver, in action at the wheel, has by far the biggest influence on efficient driving, and, through careful and considered application of specific driving techniques, the most control over it.

In short, YOU are the driving force in stretching that fuel as far as possible, bringing plenty of safety and environmental benefits along the way. Without you making some distinct, long-term changes, and adapting to a new way of thinking behind the wheel, nothing much will happen. In the driving seat this principally translates into higher levels of concentration on the job in hand, for distraction is probably the best known enemy in adapting a driving style to conserve fuel.

How far you're prepared to pursue efficient and economical driving from here is of course entirely your choice; by no means everyone wants to become – or indeed has the time or ability to become – Britain's greatest economy driver. So, in amongst all those possible shades of grey, decide on a level that suits you, prepare to take on a challenge, set yourself an achievable target, and watch your wallet benefit. Noticeable fuel economy improvements are attainable, and certainly within reach for anyone prepared to work at it, but it can be hard graft. Maximising fuel economy means taking higher than usual levels of discipline and self-control with you every time you drive your car. This in turn makes economy driving – especially in the early part of what can be a quite steep learning curve – something of an anti-social activity. Concentration levels can be such that your passengers are likely to find you don't have a lot of time for idle chat. For this reason, you might want to practice economy driving techniques alone at first, until you're feeling reasonably confident you've got the hang of it.

This is the time to concentrate on bringing more stability into your psychological makeup at the wheel. Become a less flustered, more thoughtful, patient, calm, and controlled you – a driver truly focussed on a more economical and safer driving mission whenever opportunity allows. Take a long view. Try to be more tolerant, and more philosophical in your motoring outlook. Work towards your newly chosen target every day. Use less fuel by planning and anticipating more – and reacting less.

Right now, driving efficiently to maximise economy instead of just getting from A to B will probably feel like a completely new, slightly uncomfortable, and rather alien way of motoring life, but it will get better. No matter how far along this particular road you travel, making a real difference will prove challenging, fascinating, and genuinely rewarding. You'll not only save money, but become a better driver all round, because safe and economical driving go hand in hand. Both, you might say, are simply a state of mind.

The six-point plan

In order to become a more economical, safer and more efficient driver:

• First – you'll need the right car for the job.

• Second – learn and understand the various ground rules (and occasional secrets) involved in driving any car in the most efficient and economical way. Over time these rules can usually be informed, modified, improved, and developed in light of your experience with your own vehicle.

• Third – it's time to recognise the importance of fully and properly maintaining your car.

• Fourth – your voyage of discovery will show there's plenty of helpful information out there – some of it from pretty unlikely sources – that can help you drive more economically and more efficiently. Dig it out, use it, act on it, and never stop looking for it!

• Fifth – look to the future: seek out, grasp and welcome new opportunities. Readily available modern technology can contribute greatly towards safe, efficient and economical driving.

• Sixth – take time for some soul searching, and get a grip on your emotions when in the car. Better long-term fuel economy and efficient driving generally means attuning your mental state to the job in hand – every time you get behind the wheel.

three

What are the alternatives?

In a nutshell ...
Despite the efficient driver's best efforts, the use of fossil-based fuels to move vehicles around pollutes the world's atmosphere, and one day, the world's oil supplies will, effectively, run out. Knowing these twin facts, it's long been clear that civilisation cannot continue indefinitely along the road it is presently taking. So, currently, vast amounts of effort are being expended, worldwide, to improve future vehicle environmental performance and develop new, sustainable, renewable, eco-friendly fuels to power vehicles.

Various workable alternatives already exist. Some are fully or partly oil- or other fossil-fuel-based, but may form part of an interim solution in a gradual move away from petrol/diesel. Some other currently available vehicle fuels are regarded by many as noticeably more eco-friendly than those with a fossil-related base, since they can be obtained by processing renewable sources such as plants or waste material.

A few fuels are unrelated – at least directly – to carbon-based sources, and are thus very promising as vehicle fuels of the longer-term future. Yet, as we shall see in this section, at their current stage of development, all those fuels that appear amongst the most viable future options from a vehicle standpoint, have at least some significant, sometimes controversial, and certainly far-reaching strings attached. Thats why they haven't entered widespread use so far.

In an age where technology, innovation and ingenuity are watchwords, almost no vehicle-related problem is insurmountable. Yet equally, in an age not noted for philanthropy, the massive investments needed to resolve some of the known, appreciated or anticipated problems are not yet on the horizon.

Recent years have seen increasing amounts of effort expended in the alternative-fuel field, leading to a near-future focus on electric vehicles, some interesting prototypes, a new accent on 'renewable' energy, and excited talk of low-carbon vehicles and economies. Yet early in the 21st century, short-termism abounds. The current buzz words are 'consumer incentives,' when ecological progress really depends on concerted engineering input, and a genuine desire – and stimulus – to eventually change the way of the world. Question marks hang heavily over how to truly kick-start the process of moving vehicle power sources away from today's fossil-fuel reliance, at a realistic speed.

This is not just about tomorrow's cars. The changes that must eventually be implemented to move the world away from fossil-fuel reliance are changes on a very grand and far reaching scale indeed ...

Alternative fuels – the options, and the pros and cons ...
The hybrid approach – a 'half way house' with medium term potential
Hybrids combine battery power with an internal combustion engine. As a result, they straddle the line between alternative and conventionally-fuelled vehicles. One or two well-known manufacturers have been engaged in volume production of fully practical, hybrid-powered passenger cars for some time, and others continue to work towards the launch of such vehicles. Unsurprisingly, manufacturers' interpretations of the most effective real-world solutions in such vehicles do vary, but the theme thus far has been for the driver to control the car in the normal way, while an array of hidden electronics seamlessly decides on battery charging requirements, and which source should provide motive power, in what proportions, and under what circumstances.

In such vehicles, a part of the electronic management function ensures that any power expended is not entirely wasted, with on-board batteries recharged as far as possible by the movement or braking of the vehicle rather than its internal combustion engine. In practical designs sold thus far, engine and batteries have been electronically connected, with the engine available for use both in driving the car and as a last resort to ensure the batteries remain sufficiently charged.

Hybrid drivetrains, though necessarily complex, relatively heavy, and incorporating many specialised components, have proven very practical when installed in a carefully honed 'normal' car body, offering seating and loadspace for four or five people, and all the creature comforts expected of a modern vehicle. Toyota's medium sized Prius hybrid has been particularly successful, and the principle has also been extended to the luxury 4x4 sector with some success. Using this type of hybrid approach, experience has shown that measured vehicle emissions can be significantly lower than in an equivalent car using a conventional internal combustion engine alone, with notably lower fuel consumption.

Various hybrid layouts are possible, with most production hybrids since the late 1990s utilising a relatively modest petrol engine allied to some form of automatic transmission. These have been configured in what is sometimes referred to as a 'parallel hybrid' system, alongside, and in tandem with, electric motors powered by a rechargeable battery pack. Depending on the design, drive might range from emission-free electric power only at urban speeds, through to both engine and electric motors delivering power for higher speeds or maximum acceleration.

Some 'series hybrid' cars have been experimentally developed, and this avenue is being actively explored for future production vehicles. Here, an internal combustion engine delivers power to a generator which, in outline, may then be used to both charge batteries and drive the vehicle itself via electric motors. Series hybrids have the potential to further reduce fuel consumption and provide some emission-free range, which is not always possible with parallel hybrids. Series/parallel hybrid designs are also a possibility. All such arrangements still, for the moment at least, require a conventional fuel supply, but efficiency improvements bring consumption and emissions reductions, and in some cases flexibility to charge the battery pack directly from vehicle-mounted solar cells or an external electricity source.

'Plug-in' hybrids continue the original petrol-electric (and potentially diesel-electric) theme, but allow internal batteries to be charged from the mains, giving a useful boost to the vehicle's electric-powered range, and corresponding reductions in both emissions and running costs. The first plug-in version of the Toyota Prius was launched in 2010, and because of the possibility of useful emission-free operation, the concept is becoming an electric vehicle growth area.

Hybrids at their current stage of development offer useful benefits in vehicle efficiency, but there are some strings attached, which, looking to the future, really cannot be ignored. One issue is concern about disposal of unique components at the end of their life. In the case of their latest model Prius, currently the world's most popular hybrid, Toyota claims careful

Launched in 1995, the Toyota Prius has become the world's best-selling hybrid car. From 2010, plug-in rechargeable versions began building on that success. (Courtesy Toyota GB)

planning for processing at the point of dismantling, so that disposal occurs in an environmentally responsible fashion. The manufacturer says over 85 per cent of the car can be recycled, and over 95 per cent of its materials recovered in processes accounting for approximately 2 per cent of the vehicle's full life-cycle CO_2 emissions. Special attention has been directed at ensuring efficient recycling of the vehicle's nickel-metal-hydride battery, where it's claimed 95 per cent of battery components can be recovered, with near-zero emissions.

Since 2000 diesel engine design has advanced rapidly on both emissions and consumption fronts. This has prompted several manufacturers to enter a new development phase, driven by the potential for greater fuel economy and lower CO_2 emissions in diesel-electric hybrids when compared with existing petrol-electric designs. Proposed Europe-wide reductions in average vehicle CO_2 emissions to below the 100g/km mark is focussing much interest on hybrids, as they currently represent one of few cost-effective ways to meet such limits – while maintaining the all round practicality which is taken for granted in fossil-fuel-powered cars.

Yet hybrids can really only be regarded as a stop-gap measure, their useful advantages forming a long-term bridge between the current dominance of internal combustion engines – and a future in which fossil fuels will of necessity gradually play a much reduced part. That hybrids can be more energy efficient in use than the best petrol and diesel engines alone is already proven, but while the advent of Plug-in hybrids will help, the improvements achieved in real-world use have been less clear-cut than many had hoped. For the long term, there is one ultimate drawback:

hybrids in the format we have come to understand them thus far will never be able to match the efficiency or low level emissions (at point of use) of vehicles requiring no fossil fuel supplies at all.

Existing alternative fuels
Liquefied petroleum gas (LPG)
With some adaptation and conversion, petrol engines will happily run on liquefied petroleum gas, a by-product of the long established oil extraction and petroleum refining process. LPG is a generally convenient fuel for the powering of smaller vehicles such as cars, although fuel consumption is inherently slightly higher, with a typical car achieving perhaps 80 per cent of the mpg figure delivered when using petrol. Overall performance is marginally less, though in practice this reduction is virtually unnoticeable.

LPG is a fossil-derived fuel, so its combustion inevitably results in the release of greenhouse gases – yet its use in a vehicle still has clear advantages. CO_2 emissions are typically reduced by perhaps 15 per cent to 20 per cent when compared to petrol, and there are reductions in carbon monoxide, particulate, and nitrogen oxide emissions compared to the use of diese. Lower fuel tax can ensure much reduced running costs compared to conventional fuels, even despite that slightly inferior economy. Disadvantages can include reduced loadspace, since room is required for an additional, quite bulky fuel tank. There is also a fairly limited (but growing) network of retail outlets, and the usual route to ownership is through an aftermarket vehicle conversion, since very few manufacturers offer new cars already adapted to run on LPG.

A range of authorised conversions is available for various well-known makes of vehicle, though the work involved can

Less tax brings advantageous LPG prices. Here it's 66.9 pence per litre: at the time, unleaded on the same site was 121.9 pence per litre.

make this quite an expensive process. However, converted vehicles can easily be switched to either fuel type by the driver as required, so the restricted number of LPG outlets is unlikely to cause problems, and with full tanks of both petrol and LPG, vehicle range is vastly extended. However, before opting for an LPG conversion, the first consideration should be ease of supply; there is little point in expending fuel (of whatever type) to drive some distance just to fill up! Having considered this aspect, the likely initial outlay should be carefully evaluated against the anticipated reduced fuel cost over your expected annual mileage. It's important to discover how long the cost of the conversion might take to recoup, which is when any genuine reduction in running costs will become a reality.

If you are contemplating converting a vehicle to run on LPG, before any work is undertaken, check with your insurance company about possible effects on premiums or special policy conditions, and also ensure that the work will not unduly affect or invalidate any existing manufacturer or aftermarket warranty. Bear in mind, too, that conditions may be imposed by ferry companies and the Channel Tunnel operators if you intend taking an LPG-converted vehicle to Europe.

The economy driving techniques suggested in this book can certainly be applied while using LPG as a fuel, though the reduction in consumption may not be as marked as with petrol or diesel.

More information on the use of LPG in cars, an indication of the existing LPG supply network, and a list of approved aftermarket installers is available at www.lpga.co.uk. The website www.drivelpg.co.uk offers helpful information on conversions and accredited suppliers of equipment.

Liquefied natural gas (LNG)
Whilst almost any diesel-engined vehicle could technically be converted to run on liquefied natural gas, such conversions are really only practical on larger vehicles, where some significant operational benefits are also possible.

The most significant disadvantage for smaller vehicles is the need to turn the natural gas into a liquid to make storage practical, since it must be cooled to very low temperatures, and remain in that state throughout its time in the tank of a road vehicle. This requirement makes a bulky, 'super insulated' fuel tank a necessity (following the principles of the humble vacuum thermos flask, but with considerable extra insulation). An operational tank is thus very bulky, making such an arrangement practical only on larger vans, heavy goods vehicles, and buses, where there is space to accommodate a large tank in addition to the ordinary fuel tank.

In countries where tax concessions apply to the use of natural gas-powered vehicles, overall running costs are generally lower than when using diesel, despite an LNG fuel consumption penalty of around 40 per cent. Exhaust emissions are noticeably reduced compared to diesel, although the burning of a fossil fuel comprised largely of methane inevitably still results in CO_2 being released into the atmosphere. In addition to this, any consideration of the environmental impact of using LNG as a road fuel must take into account the energy consumed in reducing the temperature of the basic product to the point where it becomes a liquid, and maintaining this temperature whilst awaiting transfer to a vehicle for use.

Compressed natural gas (CNG)

In terms of sourcing, vehicle engine modifications, chemical make up and exhaust emissions, this is a close relative of LNG, and it has proved a popular fuel in some parts of Britain and Europe.

During 2008, it was estimated that some 4 million vehicles were using CNG around the world, with Italy a leading exponent. CNG can offer up to a 20 per cent reduction in vehicle CO_2 emissions compared to petrol, though its principal advantage over LNG

and some other alternative fuels is in storage. It can be contained in tanks at high pressure but at normal ambient temperatures – in practical terms, a far less onerous demand than maintaining a tank at very low temperatures on or off a vehicle. However, because the fuel is a compressed gas but not a liquid, space for space, a tank of CNG contains significantly less than half as much energy as LNG, and perhaps 30 per cent that of diesel. This in turn leads to more rapid consumption of fuel compared to petrol or diesel, and, unless a twin-fuel on-board solution is engineered, a subsequent requirement for larger tanks. These may need to be 3 to 5 times the capacity of diesel tanks to provide similar range.

CNG combustion qualities are similar to LNG, and because of this and the need for larger storage tanks, CNG is another fuel which tends to be used most often in larger goods vehicles and buses, where space is at less of a premium than in private cars. In larger vehicles, operating cost advantages may be maximised through lower fuel taxation levels, and up to 50 per cent cheaper base prices for bulk fuel purchases. However, practical dual-fuel CNG passenger cars are available. During 2006, Citroën, for example, offered a version of its original C3 hatchback with a dual fuel option in some markets. Using CNG as its primary fuel, the car had a tank capacity of 14 cubic metres (or 11.2kg), giving a claimed gas-powered range of around 125 miles. The standard 47-litre fuel tank remained, giving a further 300 miles range, with petrol automatically selected when the gas tank was empty. Citroën claimed that fuel consumption was broadly similar on either fuel, though CO_2 emissions were 23 per cent lower in CNG mode – at 119g/km, compared with 154g/km on petrol.

LPG, LNG and CNG as existing alternative fuels

For road transport, all these fuels can offer reductions in tailpipe exhaust emissions, but all have their own advantages and disadvantages. They are at their most attractive in so called dual-fuel or bi-fuel vehicles, where an easy switch can be made between a normal fuel such as petrol or diesel, and one of the three available alternatives. However, since they hitherto have all originated as naturally occurring fossil fuels, gathered from either specific gas fields or in tandem with crude oil, their use as vehicle fuel involves the production of greenhouse gases, principally CO_2. Emissions thus remain an issue, and as with oil, supplies are finite, making their long-term use unsustainable.

LPG has proven much more appropriate as a petrol alternative for cars and small vans, and has the most advanced distribution network. The practicalities of on-board fuel storage dictate that LNG and CNG are more suited for larger vehicles, and these fuels bring a bonus of quieter running compared to diesel. Natural gas also delivers much lower nitrogen oxide emissions than diesel fuel, as well as reduced sulphur and zero particulate emissions. Overall tailpipe CO_2 emissions can be 12 to 25 per cent lower, though such figures do not take account of the not inconsiderable – but not easily quantifiable – emissions involved in the peripheral work of cooling, pressurising, processing and distributing LNG and CNG products before they reach a vehicle for use as its fuel.

In 2010, all three fuels remain available through distribution networks accessible for road vehicle use, though in Britain at least, CNG and LNG supply is largely in the hands of major fleet operators, predominantly those using large goods vehicles. Nonetheless, all three fuel distribution networks are still growing, albeit slowly in the case of both LNG and CNG. Despite the emissions advantages already mentioned, concerns about sustainability of fossil fuel supplies and the growing search for 'clean fuels' seem likely to limit their future development as practical alternatives for private cars or other small vehicles. For fleet operators, government concessions and incentives continue to influence decisions about whether any of these alternative fuels might suit any particular circumstances, and for how long.

Biogas

Whilst natural gas is a non-sustainable, fossil-based product, it is possible to produce a renewable form of natural gas that can be used as a vehicle fuel. Biogas is a mixture of methane and carbon dioxide, formed in nature through the decomposition of organic materials. All the gas resulting from this natural process thus normally escapes into the atmosphere – a concern, because methane is a much more significant greenhouse gas than carbon dioxide. However, it's possible to successfully manage biogas production on an industrial scale, using an anaerobic digester. Almost any organic material is suitable for the manufacture of biogas, including various 'energy' crops currently attracting attention as potential sources of bioethanol. Waste such as domestic refuse, and materials resulting from food manufacture, are other readily available sources, the use of which has the potential to mitigate some of the increasing difficulties faced by authorities responsible for waste disposal.

Biogas produced by these methods contains up to 70 per cent

Commercial vehicles offer space for large alternative fuel storage tanks. The CNG-powered VW Caddy EcoFuel stores 26kg of gas, providing a 270-mile range.
(Courtesy Volkswagen Commercial Vehicles)

methane; much of the rest is carbon dioxide, which must be removed under controlled conditions before the product can be used as a vehicle fuel comparable to fossil-based natural gas. The CO_2 gained during this production process is re-useable, and has commercial value. Though subject to similar practical limitations as CNG and LNG, the resulting 'uprated' natural gas is often known as biomethane or renewable natural gas (RNG), and is part of a natural cycle of 'closed loop' energy production, placing it amongst the most environmentally friendly and sustainable of all currently available vehicle fuels.

Since 2005, methane has become a new focus for research by heavy goods vehicle manufacturers, as the industry increasingly recognises the growing need to move from universal dependence on oil towards renewable fuels. The result is increasing innovation in fuel use. For example, in 2010 Volvo commenced trials of truck engines running on a mix of 25 per cent diesel fuel and 75 per cent methane gas. The company claims this capitalises on the efficiency benefits of diesel engines, while lowering both running costs and emission levels through use of methane gas as the main energy source. However, balancing this, there is notable 'external' energy consumption in consistently delivering liquid methane gas at the required temperature – around -160 degrees Celsius. Progress in selling HGVs capable of running diesel/methane fuel combinations will ultimately depend heavily on increasing methane fuel availability through expansion of the currently patchy European filling station network. As of 2010, supplies are readily available to commercial vehicle operators in Britain, but in some countries, such as Sweden, supplies are not currently available.

Biodiesel

For some time, diesel supplied in Britain has included a modest 5 per cent element of biodiesel, called 'B5,' derived from vegetable oils such as sunflower, rapeseed, or palm oil. Current diesel engines run entirely satisfactorily on B5 mixtures, and while there are environmental advantages, drivers are unlikely to see any noticeable effect on day-to-day fuel economy resulting from this low-level biodiesel element.

Though questions are increasingly being raised about biofuels generally, and the ability of today's engines and their peripheral equipment to accept higher levels of biodiesel varies dramatically, it's likely that the tolerable biodiesel proportion will rise as newer engine designs come into service. Some engines designed since 2005 can run on fuels incorporating up to 30 per cent biodiesel content, known as 'B30.' It is also possible to produce synthetic biodiesel from coal, natural gas, or biomass such as corn, sugar cane, or other plant matter.

Home production of biodiesel is possible within well-defined government limits, and various minor commercial processing facilities have been set up since 2000 to reprocess waste cooking oils, sourced from places such as restaurants and fish and chip shops, into a form of biodiesel that can be used in vehicle engines. Such outlets frequently operate at only a local level, supplying limited quantities of their product in drums that can be refilled by purchasers, rather than through traditionally-operated filling stations.

Whilst there can be distinct cost and ecological advantages in using what would otherwise be a waste product, concern over the quality is inevitable; inferior fuels may damage expensive engines that were never designed to run on high concentrations of low or variable grade fuels.

Bioethanol

Bioethanol is a genuine low-carbon fuel, which has been blended with petrol and used to power vehicles in some parts of the world since the 1970s. Its advantage in reducing reliance on crude oil supplies is proven, and it has the further advantage of presenting something approaching a 'closed loop' on CO_2 emissions, since, as they grow, the crops from which bioethanol can be produced remove much airborne carbon dioxide, some of which, of course, comes from burning the fuel in vehicle engines.

Running on high concentrations of bioethanol, an engine designed for dual-fuel use can be tuned to produce noticeably more power than petrol, though as with LPG, because of slightly lower energy density overall, fuel economy at like-for-like power levels is not normally quite as good as with petrol. A consumption increase ranging from 5 to 20 per cent might be anticipated when comparing bioethanol directly to petrol. There are also some lingering questions over reliable cold-start ability when running on high concentrations of bioethanol.

As a result of the UK government's Renewable Transport Fuel Obligation (RTFO) legislation, all modern petrol engines sold in Britain will now accept a small percentage of bioethanol in their fuel. Under the legislation, petrol supplied after 2011 must have a 5 per cent biofuel content, and a European Commission proposal already exists suggesting that by 2020 some 10 per cent of fuel used by road vehicles should be of bioethanol or biodiesel origin.

Several manufacturers already offer vehicles that can run on any mixture of unleaded petrol and bioethanol up to a maximum of 85 per cent bioethanol, known as the 'E85 standard.' Economy driving techniques can certainly be employed if the opportunity arises to use bioethanol as a fuel, though Britain currently lacks any major infrastructure for offering it to the public.

Though a line has gradually emerged between so called first and second generation biofuels, controversy increasingly surrounds the rapidly growing, worldwide demand for biologically-based transport fuels.

In some parts of the world, a switch away from less profitable agricultural food production towards crops such as sugar beet, oilseed rape, and corn intended primarily for first generation biofuels has led to accusations ranging from unsustainable de-forestation to destruction of peatlands, and raised concerns about the security and pricing of some food supplies. Second generation biofuels, produced or recycled from household and other waste products, are being viewed as a rather more enlightened and acceptable alternative, but there are nonetheless calls from some quarters for western governments to think again about recently agreed subsidies aimed at further promoting the use of biofuels generally.

Saab introduced E85 bioethanol-powered cars to Britain in 2006. Limited supplies of the fuel have been made available via the Morrisons supermarket chain.

Future alternative fuels
Electricity – alternative one
Experiments to develop successful, electrically-powered vehicles have been going on almost since motor cars were invented and electricity harnessed for the good of mankind.

Many perfectly workable electric vehicles have been built in the last 100 years, though the surge of interest in electricity to power private cars, trams, and trolleybuses in the first part of the twentieth century had all but petered out by the 1950s. The ecological pressures of more recent times have rapidly rekindled interest in electricity as a potential private vehicle power source, but despite renewed efforts and 21st century advanced technology, some particularly stubborn problems are delaying widespread public acceptance.

At their present state of development, road-going electric vehicles in general perform best in predominantly short to medium distance, lower speed use on a regular daily cycle. In such circumstances they can offer zero emissions at the point of use, where 'on the spot' fuel consumption is also effectively zero, leading to very low environmental and running costs for the end user. These are great benefits in cities and urban areas, beating conventional vehicles hands-down. For drivers happy to accept some quite specific compromises, or where usage patterns exploit the advantageous characteristics of existing electric vehicles and their charging methods and times, they can be extremely useful, and seemingly very fuel and emissions efficient.

The downside is that electric vehicles overall are only slowly moving towards the familiar and comfortable balance of practicality, range, performance, and all round ease

of use that have gradually become indispensable hallmarks of vehicles powered by internal combustion engines. And as we shall see, issues with the vehicles themselves are just a part of the overall ecological story.

Today, perfectly usable all-electric cars, commercial vehicles, and even motorcycles are on sale, but all are modest-volume products with at least some disadvantages when compared to vehicles powered by petrol or diesel engines. On a practical level, the biggest concern is probably user 'range anxiety' – the constant worry of having a limited range available, and a discharged battery at a time when the vehicle is urgently required, with local recharging involving significant delay. Years of development in battery technology have brought full recharge time claims down to periods anywhere between an hour and overnight, but this is still a sharp contrast with the few minutes needed to refill conventional fuel tanks.

Other consumer-related issues centre on modest roadgoing performance, and the comparatively limited range available, even when a battery pack is fully charged. At the heart of all these problems is battery technology, which despite years of effort and gradual improvement, remains the single most important factor in the reluctance of mainstream manufacturers to commence volume production of practical electric cars. In this sense, practical means comparable with modern petrol or diesel vehicles in areas that matter most to customers. They include initial price and cost-effectiveness, size, seating capacity, safety, weight, potential useful range and time to refuel, acceleration characteristics, and the ability to sustain cruising speeds beyond those found in urban areas over long distances.

Major manufacturers' electric car pricing reflects the investment involved. At launch in 2010, including grant aid, the list price of the small Mitsubishi i-MIEV was £33,000.

Balancing these drawbacks, electricity has gained a reputation as a non-polluting and thus clean 'fuel.' This is perfectly true at the point of use, but as things stand it's neither clean – nor sustainable – overall. The problem here is in generation of electricity to charge vehicle batteries. Although the proportion of electricity delivered by clean alternative sources such as wind, solar, and tidal methodologies is rising, electricity production today tends to bring with it some direct emissions production, resulting from consumption of fossil fuel – coal, gas or oil – to power a generator. Because this occurs distant from the point of vehicle use, the fuel consumed and emissions involved in delivering a battery charge cannot be known to an electric vehicle user, and tend to be forgotten – but, though diverted away from the vehicle, there's no getting away from it – fossil fuel consumption and pollution remain a

fact of life in generating most of today's electricity.

Improvements offsetting known emissions problems can certainly be anticipated. For instance, the proportion of electricity derived from 'green' sources is slowly rising, and nuclear power seems set to reappear on the agenda. Future conventional electricity generation will be less polluting than in the past, as coal fired power stations start to benefit from so-called 'clean coal' and 'carbon capture' technology. Yet continuing to source most electricity in this way for the foreseeable future then begs more questions about sustainability ...

If most or all of the disadvantages inherent in today's electric vehicles could be resolved, and drivers currently using fossil-fuel powered vehicles were motivated to switch to electricity en-masse, demand seems likely to sky-rocket. The energy extracted daily from petrol or diesel in the tanks of millions of vehicles would then come instead from millions of vehicle batteries – each requiring manufacture, and a large number requiring a periodic – probably daily – recharge to keep the vehicle mobile. Even assuming the increase in diverted pollution already mentioned could be effectively dealt with at electricity generating stations, any widespread switch in vehicle motive power away from fossil fuels and towards electricity could hardly fail to bring increased demand for additional generation capability. So, another question arises: without significant investment, where would that be found?

One balancing factor here is improved efficiency: using an electric motor as a primary source of movement immediately makes electric vehicles more efficient in fuel use overall for the distance travelled than their petrol and diesel counterparts. Studies have suggested that, typically, perhaps 20 per cent to 25 per cent of the energy released from its fuel by an internal combustion engine ends up actually driving the vehicle. With an electric motor, that figure may reach 80 per cent. In isolation, this differential weighs very clearly in favour of more extensive use of electric vehicles in future, since more efficient 'engines' will need far less 'fuel' to move them around. This in turn should naturally result in lower emissions at the point of electricity generation.

It might, but things are not quite this straightforward. As we've seen, in most circumstances, a fuel such as electricity discharged from storage batteries is unlike established liquid fuels, in that, with limited exceptions, its use has *already* required consumption of fuel – and emissions have been generated as a result. If, however, the power used for vehicle battery charging could be generated entirely from 'clean' sources, and the vehicles involved are indeed 80 per cent efficient in converting electricity into movement, then such vehicles will, by default, win hands down any competition over both consumption and pollution levels. The trouble is, early in the 21st century the gulf between obtaining sufficient electricity to power all Britain's (and ultimately the world's) future vehicles entirely from 'clean' sources – and the reality of today's quite inefficient and largely fossil-fuel powered electricity generating situation is vast.

Controversial questions about what type of fuel might power future generation capacity – and exactly how much capacity would be needed – are thus central to the future of genuine, 'closed loop' zero-emitting electric vehicles. Whilst electricity originating from 'green' sources is fast gaining an impetus, the industry designing and manufacturing the equipment required has hardly come of age. The front running, most practical source for provision of 'clean' electricity so far has emerged as the wind turbine: experience has shown putting such facilities in place is a long-term task – which comes with its own related manufacturing, environmental, social and political issues and concerns – most of them far removed from electric vehicle considerations in isolation.

A number of wider aspects of using electricity to power large numbers of future road vehicles are worth mentioning here. What, for instance, would be the overall impact of very significant levels of high capacity battery production on consumption of the world's resources? Logic suggests seemingly little point in switching from depletion of one non-sustainable resource, such as oil, into depletion of another, such as lead, or lithium or manganese – each with their own unique problems and distinctly finite supply limitations – in order to produce vast numbers of vehicle batteries or other components. Questions also arise over the extent of inherent recyclability or actual disposal of such products as they reach end-of-life: new infrastructures will be needed to deal with what could well become rapidly increasing numbers of unique component parts from electric vehicles.

Vehicles powered solely by electricity will naturally require some convenient and widespread infrastructure to allow recharging. At its heart this problem centres on the safety and practicality issues involved in facilitating potentially quite lengthy periods of vehicle battery charging at or near the roadside. Promising trials led by British companies commenced in 2008 to provide modest scale local area arrangements for electric vehicle charging, and a number of companies are working on or have already demonstrated practical roadside systems. Ambitious plans have since emerged from the Energy Technology Institute to provide charging points – including payment and appropriate 'safe-access' technology – in several of Britain's major cities, founded on the expectation of at least 50,000 electric vehicles on British roads by 2015. Similar plans are moving forward in parts of Europe.

Set against this, the implications for additional street clutter as a result of a fast-growing electric vehicle charging network, and the difficulties of providing parking space to allow charging to occur in crowded town centres, are already clear.

One alternative to this 'kerbside charging' approach being actively explored is the rapid change-over of replaceable battery packs. Here, a stock of charged packs are held in

Safe, practical charging stations are vital for electric vehicles. Installation of suitable key-operated connecting points is already under way in some cities across Europe. (Courtesy Elektrobay)

a 'filling station,' awaiting vehicles requiring a battery swap. With careful vehicle design and robotised operation, this might be accomplished in a few minutes, broadly comparable to filling a fuel tank. Prototype vehicles exist, and battery-changeover stations have been promised in Tokyo and Denmark.

Whilst the concept initially appears quite convenient, it does raise immediate questions ranging from ensuring compatibility across different manufacturers' vehicles, to the commercial viability of what would ultimately have to become a worldwide operation – in the face of other, competing – maybe simpler – charging alternatives. Given today's established and convenient 'one type suits all' filling station structure, a simple, standard plug-in-anywhere charging solution requiring no special facilities, or major investments does seem attractive. As electric vehicle designs develop, a simple, standardised plug-in charging approach already seems to have something of an air of inevitability about it ...

When compared to petrol- or diesel-powered vehicles, electric vehicles present some new safety issues. Recent development has been so rapid that during 2009 the International Standards Organisation (ISO) was prompted to issue new safety standards for electric, hybrid and fuel cell-powered vehicles, relating to on-board rechargeable energy storage and propulsion systems, driving and parking requirements, and protection against certain specific electric vehicle hazards.

Meanwhile, a different safety problem concerns noise. Electric vehicles tend to be very quiet in operation, particularly at low speeds and when pulling away, situations where pedestrians have become very accustomed to noticeable and recognisable engine noise. Remove those familiar sounds, and people may be unaware a vehicle is close by – bringing attendant risks and dangers, especially to children, the blind or hard of hearing. This problem has stimulated high-level industry and government discussion, in Britain, Europe the US and Japan, regarding the introduction of minimum vehicle noise levels. After years spent by designers and legislators reducing vehicle noise, this might seem a retrograde step, but we all rely instinctively on hearing vehicles coming for everyday tasks like crossing the road. Given the likely growth in electric vehicle numbers, the broadcast of a characteristic, electronically generated 'sound signature' has been suggested as a possible solution in urban environments, fading away as speeds rise.

Despite the various disadvantages outlined here, electric vehicles remain one of the two most promising avenues for the eventual replacement of fossil-fuel powered vehicles. If there is an overriding message in this brief review of the situation, it is surely that electric vehicles are not, as yet, a wide-scale panacea: objective analysis shows more to consider than the much-trumpeted headline 'point of use' zero emissions benefits. The cycle of consumption events, the emissions created, the vehicle mechanical makeup, the materials consumed, the emissions generated, and the difficulties involved in manufacture, operation, maintenance and disposal of electric vehicles add up to something very different from the cycle established by today's conventional cars – but something that, ecologically speaking, really cannot be ignored.

Development work continues apace, with major manufacturers working towards electric vehicles capable of a 300 mile range – at realistic speeds for longer distance travel. Set against over 100 years of internal combustion engine development, recent progress has been rapid: an electric car revolution seems closer than ever, while remaining, tantalisingly, just out of reach. Quite apart from the sustainability issues, the key breakthroughs in practicality and direct all round comparability with existing vehicles, together so vital to bring electric cars conclusively into the mainstream, remain frustratingly elusive.

Maybe vehicle users will have to adapt and change instead. Or could hydrogen power be the answer?

Hydrogen – alternative 2
Hydrogen as a fuel, and fuel cell vehicles (FCVs)

A number of manufacturers have reached low volume or trial production of vehicles – including two-wheelers – capable of running on hydrogen. Such vehicles can have attractive exhaust emission advantages, as water is the only significant by-product when using hydrogen to power a fuel cell operated vehicle, effectively reducing harmful emissions at the point of use to zero.

Hydrogen thus appears as a tempting alternative fuel. However, oil, the basis of today's fuels, contains the energy needed to power our vehicles as it comes out of the ground, while equivalent natural reserves of accessible hydrogen don't exist – at least on planet Earth. There are very abundant supplies of hydrogen around, locked away in water, but extracting it requires consumption of quite a lot of energy – before using it to power a vehicle. After production, Hydrogen presents other energy-consuming problems in distribution and storage. Practical amounts of hydrogen can be stored only as a liquid at very low temperature (typically -250 degrees C) and at a pressure of 3-5 bar (up to 60lb/sq in) or as a compressed gas at more normal atmospheric temperatures – but higher pressures; or at some compromise levels midway between such extremes.

Significant energy consumption is involved in changing temperatures and pressures of the gas to such an extent, and in maintaining temperature-controlled transport and storage, say at a filling station. Hydrogen in vehicle storage tanks must also be maintained in similar conditions when the vehicle is unused, potentially for days or even weeks at a time.

Maintaining hydrogen as a liquid is a possibility, but, unless further energy is used to prevent it, the liquid turns naturally to highly inflammable gas as its temperature rises. Storage as a gas seems more appropriate for vehicles, though the tanks needed to provide adequate range on existing prototypes tend to be quite large – of perhaps 150 to 200 litres, and also able to withstand significant internal pressures – raising entirely separate questions about leakage – and space available on board vehicles. The highly inflammable nature of the fuel stock also raises questions about safety in vehicles parked for any length of time, and specific measures will be needed to provide for safe, secure storage in the event of major vehicle collisions or serious on-board equipment failures.

This situation brings further questions over how a practical worldwide hydrogen distribution network might be developed. There are a handful of (non-commercial) hydrogen filling stations in Britain, limited numbers of experimental stations exist in Germany, and there are numbers in California and Japan, where hydrogen-powered vehicle trials continue. However, there is presently little incentive to roll out any far-reaching network – until significant numbers of vehicles exist to make use of it.

The problems outlined above resulting from a 'network-distribution' approach may be overcome by simply producing the required amount of hydrogen on the spot, using either electricity or natural gas for 'one vehicle at a time' refuelling. Though development of suitable systems is at a very early stage, this notably less energy-intensive approach is under active consideration and in UK development at the time of writing, and – long-term sustainability issues apart – appears to have the potential to avoid most of the costly distribution infrastructure problems described earlier.

Hydrogen overall thus emerges as a fuel with much potential, but some hidden pitfalls. Nonetheless, technology exists, or is being developed, to cope with known or anticipated problems, so, the biggest question is: where might the extra energy to produce and possibly distribute the fuel actually come from? As with the energy needed to charge electrically-powered vehicle batteries, the obvious answer – in theory at least – involves renewable or sustainable resources. Unlike fossil-based oil, a virtually infinite, virtually pollution free hydrogen supply could become available for vehicle fuel – if renewable energy sources such as solar, wind, wave or hydro-electric power were alone used to manufacture and distribute it.

Unfortunately, the availability situation here is similar to that for electric vehicles. Vast amounts of hydrogen would ultimately be needed to power vehicles worldwide, and new methods of producing or obtaining it may well appear – but current commercial production methods involve either consumption of non-sustainable natural gas, or electrolysis to release hydrogen from water – with the prerequisite of not inconsiderable amounts of electricity being available first. This, in another classic swings and roundabouts situation, raises questions about the scale of electricity generation needed to deliver the substantial hydrogen volumes required. Even allowing for improved efficiency, of perhaps 60 per cent compared to the 18 to 24 per cent of today's internal combustion engines, a medium term switch to equivalent numbers of

hydrogen-powered vehicles covering similar distances to today's vehicles would place new demands on the world's ability to generate the additional electricity needed.

Thus, if hydrogen emerged as a vehicle fuel of choice, before it could become truly practical and sustainable, powering the numbers of vehicles using petrol and diesel today, new ways of producing hydrogen – or major upgrades in electricity generation capacity – seem inescapable. Just as with electric vehicles already mentioned, given the current rate of facility growth, far from all of that new power could originate from renewable supplies for some considerable time to come.

Yet overall, in spite of the anticipated difficulties today, hydrogen still holds potential promise as a vehicle fuel, with some manufacturers suggesting it may yet prove to be the only practical alternative fuel of the future. With ongoing European legislation focussing more on lowering actual vehicle exhaust emissions towards zero – hydrogen's biggest advantage – than on dealing with, and effectively disposing of, the resulting diverted emissions – an integral and inevitable part of generating the electricity needed using today's technology – experimental work continues.

However, in the absence of sufficient 'clean' energy sources, or viable alternative ways to produce the gas, the ecological irony of going through the tortuous, fuel consuming and emissions-burdened process of generating significant amounts of electricity to create, distribute and store hydrogen – which is then consumed to generate smaller quantities of electricity to actually power a vehicle – has not been lost on more astute commentators ...

Hydrogen-powered vehicles today

Two main development themes have become apparent amongst manufacturers working on hydrogen-powered vehicles: one is the adaptation of petrol engines to enable them to run on hydrogen; the other is to generate electricity to power a vehicle electric motor (or motors) by utilising hydrogen in an on-board fuel cell.

A leading exponent in the first group has been German manufacturer BMW, which has invested some twenty years of development work in the BMW 'Hydrogen 7' engine, despite which its long-term future now seems uncertain. Fitted into a version of the company's 7 Series model line, the 12 cylinder, 260 horsepower, internal combustion engine is capable of running on hydrogen or petrol, delivering similar power with either fuel. Low volume production began in 2006, and vehicles have been demonstrated worldwide in extended high-profile trials. The manufacturers claim a switch is possible at any time from hydrogen to conventional petrol power, and the car can accelerate from zero to 62mph in 9.5 seconds, with a top speed of 143mph. A normal 74-litre petrol tank is fitted, plus an additional tank holding up to 8 kilograms of liquid hydrogen: a cruising range of over 125 miles is claimed on hydrogen, plus a further 300 miles under petrol power. The vehicle can thus still be used normally when no hydrogen is on board, though the usual emissions penalties of a large petrol engine then remain. Running on hydrogen, no CO_2 is produced, with the fuel itself contributing little to exhaust emissions: however because hydrogen is burnt using air drawn from the atmosphere –

Seen at a Berlin filling point, this BMW 7 series dual-fuel, hydrogen-powered saloon appears indistinguishable from its conventional counterparts. (Courtesy BMW Group)

in what remains a largely conventional internal combustion engine – some other unwanted exhaust emissions do result. Though actual levels are low, the most noteworthy undesirable product is Nitrogen Oxide.

The possibilities of fuel cells as a power source date back to ideas set out in the mid 1800s, but it wasn't until the 1980s that the motor industry started to explore their potential in detail. Today such systems operate on a principle of combining hydrogen with oxygen from the air, using a catalyst such as platinum, to produce electricity. Prototype vehicle fuel cells already deliver sufficient energy to operate quite powerful electric motors, well capable of driving a car. Acceleration and top speeds achieved in prototype vehicles are claimed to be comparable with those delivered by current petrol and diesel cars, while noise levels are much lower.

A cooperative venture between British company Intelligent Energy and Japanese motorcycle manufacturer Suzuki has resulted in trials of prototype hydrogen-fuelled scooters. (Courtesy Suzuki GB PLC)

Nissan, Honda, Ford and General Motors are amongst the car manufacturers in the group investigating a fuel cell approach, with vehicles in development or under lease in modest numbers to carefully selected customers. Meanwhile, a successful partnership between UK-based technology company Intelligent Energy and Japanese motorcycle manufacturer Suzuki has resulted in a fuel cell-powered version of the Suzuki Burgman two-wheeler. First presented at the 2009 Tokyo Motor Show, the prototype machine can be fuelled from a hydrogen cylinder in just a few minutes, giving a range of approximately 220 miles (350 km), comparable to that offered by a conventionally powered Burgman scooter.

Since the 1990s, progress in fuel cell design and evolution has been rapid. Honda showed what became its 'FCX Clarity' prototype as a concept in 2005, and just two years later working examples existed. The company's handful of roadgoing prototypes, running in Japan and the US during 2009, have 170-litre hydrogen fuel tanks giving a claimed range of around 300 miles, and hydrogen fuel consumption said to be equivalent to around 100mpg on fossil fuel. Other manufacturers operating prototype vehicles in the same period have claimed working consumption figures hovering around 1kg of hydrogen providing enough energy for between 15 and 50 miles of travel.

Today, experimental hydrogen-powered vehicles continue trials on a daily, real-world basis around the globe. Some advanced prototypes have covered many hundreds of thousands of miles – and in use are reported in many ways to be almost indistinguishable from fossil-fuel powered production cars. These prototypes, from some of the world's leading car manufacturers,

Honda's 'FCV Clarity' fuel cell-powered prototypes have operated successfully on hydrogen for some years, but remain distant from mass production.

represent current state of the art, yet remain distant from series production. Various issues are absorbing much development time. Dependent on the chosen method of hydrogen use and its storage, these issues include the cost, complexity and practicality of the on-board processes involved, finding easy ways to mass-produce workable fuel cell designs, arranging for fail-safe standby power sources, and ensuring reliable starting and operation in cold conditions. Another significant worry is the issue of hydrogen cars' overall energy efficiency and sustainability as outlined earlier. On a more practical note the absence of any widespread distribution infrastructure or workable

alternative method of providing hydrogen fuel to vehicle users seems likely to remain a stumbling block for some time.

In current approaches to hydrogen-powered cars, significant weight is added and space stolen to provide storage tanks for amounts of hydrogen sufficient to provide an acceptable range. Also, as we've seen, storage may require a controlled environment far removed from normal atmospheric conditions, and because of this and the volatile nature of hydrogen generally, complete road-user safety in the event of any leakages or serious accidents must also of necessity be closely considered.

Amongst the list of problem areas, overall energy efficiency is perhaps the biggest issue facing hydrogen. As a vehicle fuel it has already been proved to be workable – but it's hardly sustainable if its use is likely to involve the consumption of more energy overall – to move the vehicle and keep it fuelled – than the existing fossil-fuel powered equivalent it is intended to replace.

Here, the modest rate of development of 'green' electricity sources returns to haunt the hydrogen equation. Given the scale and range of problems still ahead, some promising hydrogen-based projects have already been cancelled, and most manufacturers currently operating hydrogen-powered prototypes admit to running other alternative-fuel programmes and prototypes in tandem.

Other 'wild card' possibilities for alternative fuels

Promising work has been undertaken since 2005 on researching biofuel production from waterborne algae. One of the leading exponents of fuel production by this method is Colorado-based Solix Biofuels Inc, a company which emerged from elements of the US department of Energy's 'Aquatic Species Program,' dating back as far as 1978. Today the company is marketing quantities of micro-algae based bio-crude oil, which can be refined into a form of diesel fuel for vehicles.

In 2002 Guildford-based company, TMO Renewables, was set up to explore production of Ethanol from bacteria. If the process under development proves workable and exploitable commercially, Ethanol production by this method could play a future part in negating the various controversies centred on the growing of food products for biofuels, and related deforestation. A demonstration plant has been assembled in Surrey, with a view to finding worldwide buyers for the process and its associated technology.

Road vehicles have been produced in very limited numbers powered by compressed air, either directly or involving use of electric motors, and a number of companies have been set up since the 1990s in attempts to develop the technology. Whilst use of compressed air in this way has been demonstrated as workable at prototype level, various attempts to start series production have fallen by the wayside. The concept in any case raises sustainability questions over the necessary energy consumption involved in compressing the air, before it can be used as a vehicle fuel.

So, what of the alternatives?

In the early 21st century, looking objectively at the potential for efficient motoring in future years, plenty of opportunities exist for reductions in the use of fossil-based fuels. For the longer term, whilst breakthroughs can and do happen, it seems only electricity and hydrogen hold genuine promise as practical, potentially sustainable vehicle fuels of the future. Each of the alternatives now being used, or pursued, as vehicle fuels present different problems and challenges, but the biggest longer term problems for electricity and hydrogen lie outside the vehicles themselves in finding – or developing – an efficient, ecologically-friendly way to generate the electricity they need, directly or indirectly, to make them both acceptably practical and fully viable.

The future: where do efficient drivers go from here?

Since the enormity of the twin costs of steadily declining oil reserves and the polluting effects of vehicle (and other) exhaust emissions have become more fully appreciated, European legislation has been one of the most dominant forces worldwide in ensuring vehicle exhausts become cleaner and engines generally more economical at the design level.

Although low-emission hybrid vehicles are making inroads, vast sums continue to be invested by private car manufacturers around the world in developing what are effectively still conventional petrol and diesel engines in order to achieve legislators' demands.

European regulations have existed for some time intended to reduce car CO_2 emissions to an average of 130g/km per car by 2015, but during 2008 the European Parliament approved new European Commission plans for still tighter restrictions. If enacted as drafted, these would invoke an average CO_2 emissions limit of 120g/km, applying to 65 per cent of bigger manufacturers' new cars from January 2012 – rising gradually to 100 per cent from 2015. A derogation in the draft plans, for manufacturers producing under 300,000 cars a year, would require their average 'fleet' emission to reduce by 25 per cent compared to 2007 figures – a very significant demand for smaller manufacturers, who tend to produce some of the more powerful, highest emitting – and least economical – vehicles currently available. Such regulations could prove stringent enough to lead to a step change in the mix of new vehicles sold in Europe, with smaller, more economical vehicles then decisively becoming the dominant force.

Whilst ever-tightening future legislation thus holds the prospect of increasingly tough targets for vehicle makers, efficient drivers will be ideally placed to reap the benefits. Amongst the vehicles arriving in response to changing legislation in the next few years, it's already certain new, more advanced hybrid and full-electric vehicles will be amongst them, coming to the market as manufacturers seek to rein in, and then lower, their average emission figures.

End game

To fully address issues of genuine sustainability and low atmospheric pollution, it seems the world's future goal – and not just in transport – must be to progress towards economies based on zero carbon emissions. Research for this book suggests that, early in the 21st century, thats little more than an idealistic target, unlikely to be achieved any time soon, if ever. Realistically, many years of (hopefully declining) carbon emissions lie ahead in pursuit of that target.

For vehicle users, regulation through legislation as outlined above is well and good – so long as prices don't sky-rocket, and design potential exists to continue reducing vehicle exhaust emissions and improving fuel consumption over time. Yet the law of diminishing returns will ultimately determine workable limits in both areas, for in a the primary function of powering a vehicle, engines must of necessity also remain practical for everyday use – a balancing act set to become progressively more difficult. Car buyers expect adequate performance, greater refinement, more equipment and improved safety standards – but, as the efficient driver may have noticed, these demands involve an unwelcome trend. Passenger cars today are becoming heavier, potentially needing more power and thus more fuel – just to deliver on those steadily spiralling expectations ...

For the future something has to change. So far, innovation, talent and skill amongst vehicle and engine designers and manufacturers have continued to deliver lowered emissions and improved fuel consumption in the face of mounting challenges, but as scope to continue balancing this equation gradually becomes more limited, so change is inevitable. At some stage, conventional engines seem destined to be permanently relegated to a secondary, high-economy, lower power, lower emissions function as auxiliary or battery-charging power units in notably more efficient hybrid or electric vehicles – a process which has already begun. Smaller, ever more economical, low pollution internal combustion engines could thus have a vital but gradually declining role in passenger cars for years to come.

Vehicles powered entirely by electricity hold a long-term promise, and continued active pursuit of alternative 'clean' vehicle fuels – amongst which, early in the 21st century, hydrogen seems the only serious contender – may yet result in new technological achievements. Meanwhile, ecologically efficient bio-fuel, despite some controversy, could become a vital cornerstone in a medium-term bridge between yesterday's fossil-fuelled power units – and those new vehicle engines or fuels of the future. Nothing here is settled: the future of motoring could still turn on breakthrough development of different types of power units – or different types of fuels.

What is becoming clear is that there is now more development time and effort behind the internal combustion engine than lies ahead of it. In the form we have come to know them, petrol and diesel engines inevitably consume some carbon-based fuel, and so can never be totally emission-free – or entirely sustainable. So, after more than a hundred years of sterling service, such engines are moving,

imperceptibly, towards a golden sunset. Yet even so, a dramatic change in vehicle motive power units – particularly at the commercial vehicle end of the scale – still seems much less likely than a very gradual shift from one fuel type to another over time.

Its no exaggeration to say motorised transport in its many forms nowadays lies at the very heart of developed society – but it's also true that the growing pressures of an increasingly eco-friendly approach to transport will make significant change inevitable. Entrenched attitudes must undergo a fundamental shift if the levels of mobility regarded by civilisation as normal early in the 21st century are to be sustained indefinitely. While transport is far from alone in consuming resources or contaminating the atmosphere, these changes will be driven by dwindling oil supplies, rising pollution and the importance of resource conservation – all set to become key issues during this century.

With a Climate Change Act target requiring Britain to reduce carbon emissions to 34 per cent below 1990 levels by 2020, and to 80 per cent below by 2050, the scope and the scale of this issue is vast, and it will embrace many other aspects of society beyond transport. Today's efficient drivers are already working towards a more ecologically-acceptable tomorrow, but reductions of such magnitude will rely on the unshakeable determination of future governments, testing the strength of political will around the world in coming years. Big, costly, far-sighted, ecologically driven decisions lie ahead as the world's hundred year era of reliance on fossil fuels to power its planes and trains, ships, trucks and automobiles enters its final phase.

four

Appendix

Government information and advice on efficient driving and related taxation and legislation
Information on the latest UK rules relating to vehicle taxation and current tax rates, and a range of other motoring related information and advice is available at
www.direct.gov.uk/motoring

A booklet providing emission and fuel consumption figures for all new cars available in Britain, together with a range of related information, is published by the Vehicle Certification Agency (VCA) and is available at www.vca.gov.uk

The VCA's Car Fuel Database at www.vcacarfueldata.org.uk can be searched based on vehicle fuel economy, tax band, or by individual car make or model.

The Department For Transport has a comprehensive website covering legislation-related aspects of motoring at www.dft.gov.uk

A special section relates to efficient driving called 'Act on CO_2.' This can be found at www.dft.gov.uk/ActOnCO2

An eco-safe driving style is promoted by the Driving Standards Agency at www.dsa.gov.uk
This can best be accessed by a search on the site using the words 'eco-safe'.

Much helpful background information on driving safely for economy, together with updates on current emissions and biofuel-related legislation, is available on the Department for Transport website (or via links from the site) at www.direct.gov.uk/en/Environmentandgreenerliving/Greenertravel/DG_064428

Sharing a car
Many County Councils and Unitary authorities participate in and encourage car sharing schemes to encourage more efficient vehicle use. Local authority websites usually contain details of operational schemes. The website www.liftshare.com covers

lift sharing by car, cycling and taxi. In 2010 it claimed over 350,000 registered members.

Manuals and handbooks
Various specialists offer handbooks for vehicles of the past at
www. manualsource.co.uk
www.pooksmotorbooks.co.uk
www.instruction-manuals.co.uk
www.carhandbooks.co.uk
In addition to a handbook, drivers of older vehicles might feel a workshop manual would be helpful. A range of such publications is available at
www.haynes.co.uk
The suppliers mentioned above may also be able to help with manuals.

Motor industry information
The Society of Motor Manufacturers and Traders (SMMT) offers information concerning fuel economy and emissions at www.smmt.co.uk
Booklets entitled *Drive Green, Drive Safely* and *New Car CO$_2$ Report* are available to download.

Alternative fuels information
More information on the use of liquid petroleum gas (LPG) as a vehicle fuel, an indication of the existing LPG supply network and a list of approved aftermarket installers is available at
www.uklpga.co.uk
Information on LPG vehicle conversions and accredited suppliers of the equipment required can be found at
www.drivelpg.co.uk
Information on biofuel production from waterborne algae is available at
www.solixbiofuels.com

General advice
Some other helpful websites offering

eco-driving tips, or efficient driving material in general –
www.theaa.com
www.rac.co.uk
www.racfoundation.org
www iam.org.uk
www.est.org.uk
The Green Car website offers news and information, vehicle tests and listings of interest to efficient drivers at
www.thegreencarwebsite.co.uk
A similar consumer-oriented site concerned with emissions and pollution issues is at www.cleangreencars.co.uk
Get regular updates on the cheapest fuel prices around the country as well as some fuel saving tips at
www.petrolprices.com
Extensive live UK traffic information and a number of related travel services such as mobile navigation can be found at www.trafficmaster.co.uk
Drivers looking to plan particularly economical routes or journeys may find helpful information at
www.viamichelin.co.uk
The Environmental Transport Association has a helpful website at
www.eta.co.uk
The Highways Agency (HA) website offers helpful information concerning repair and maintenance work on the British main road network. Extensive coverage of lane and road closures is provided, with updates at appropriate intervals. E-mail alerts are available on the progress of longer-term projects. Full details of all HA services can be found at www.highways.gov.uk
The HA also operates a digital-only radio station, offering detailed traffic information on a daily basis. 'Traffic Radio' is broadcast on DAB digital radio. It is also available on the internet, at www.trafficradio.org.uk

Index

Save 30%*
on RAC Breakdown Cover.

As a thank you for purchasing your product from RAC, we'd like to offer you 30% off RAC Breakdown Cover.

Here for you 24/7

With RAC you get the peace of mind of knowing we're here to help you 24 hours a day, 365 days a year. We have more patrols per member† than any other breakdown service, so we can find you and fix your problem fast.

If you ever run into trouble on the road, you couldn't be in better hands. And now when you join you'll be better off too, with your 30% discount.

Rest assured with RAC

– Personal based cover – as a driver or passenger in any vehicle**

– Our diagnostic computers start working on your problem from the moment you call

– We aim to reach you within 40 minutes on average and fix 80% of problems on the spot, fast^

– We'll follow you for a while once we've got you going again, just to make sure everything's OK.

To join RAC today for 30% less,
call 0800 716 976 and quote DT0440
Calls may be recorded and/or monitored.
or visit rac.co.uk